French Grammar

Beginner, Intermediate, and Advanced Levels

Third Edition

by

Christopher Kendris, Ph.D.

*Diplômé, Faculté des Lettres, Université de Paris et Institut
de Phonétique, Paris (en Sorbonne)*
Certificat, Ecole Pédagogique de l'Alliance Française de Paris
B.S., M.S., Columbia University in the City of New York
M.A., Ph.D., Northwestern University in Evanston, Illinois

Former Chairman
Department of Foreign Languages
Farmingdale High School
Farmingdale, New York

Theodore Kendris, Ph.D.

Ph.D., Université Laval, Québec, Canada

Adjunct Instructor
Luzerne County Community College

BARRON'S

BARRON'S EDUCATIONAL SERIES, INC.

To St. Sophia Greek Orthodox Church
of Albany, New York, our parish

and

To the eternal memory of our beloved
Ariadne-Yolanda Kendris,
who is always by our side

With love

All inquiries should be addressed to:
Barron's Educational Series, Inc.
250 Wireless Boulevard
Hauppauge, New York 11788
http:www.barronseduc.com

Library of Congress Catalog Control No. 2010931195

ISBN: 978-0-7641-4595-7

PRINTED IN CHINA
9

Table of Contents

About the Authors   viii
How to Use This Book   x
Preface   xi

The Basics, Beginner Level

§1. GUIDE TO PRONOUNCING FRENCH
    SOUNDS   1
§2. CAPITALIZATION, PUNCTUATION
    MARKS, AND WORD DIVISION   5
    2.1   Capitalization   5
    2.2   Punctuation Marks   5
    2.3   Word Division   6

The Parts of Speech

§3. ARTICLES, Beginner Level   9
    3.1   Definite Article   9
    3.2   Indefinite Article   13
    3.3   Partitive   14
§4. NOUNS, Beginner Level   17
    4.1   Gender   17
    4.2   Plural of Nouns—The Basics   20
§5. ADJECTIVES, Beginner Level   21
    5.1   Formation   21
    5.2   Agreement   23
    5.3   Position   24
    5.4   Types   25
        5.4–1   Descriptive   25
        5.4–2   Demonstrative   25
        5.4–3   Interrogative   26

	5.4–4	Possessive	26
	5.4–5	Comparative and Superlative	28
	5.4–6	*Meilleur* and *Mieux*	31
	5.4–7	Adjectives Used in an Adverbial Sense	31
§6.	PRONOUNS, Beginner, Intermediate, and Advanced Levels		32
6.1	Types		32
	6.1–1	Subject Pronouns	32
	6.1–2	Direct Object Pronouns	33
	6.1–3	Indirect Object Pronouns	34
	6.1–4	Double Object Pronouns	35
	6.1–5	*En*	35
	6.1–6	*Y*	36
	6.1–7	Disjunctive Pronouns	37
	6.1–8	Demonstrative Pronouns	38
	6.1–9	Indefinite Pronouns	40
	6.1–10	Interrogative Pronouns	41
	6.1–11	Possessive Pronouns	43
	6.1–12	Reflexive Pronouns	44
	6.1–13	Relative Pronouns	45
	6.1–14	*C'est* + adjective + *à* + infinitive	47
	6.1–15	*Il est* + adjective + *de* + infinitive	47
	6.1–16	Neuter Pronoun *le*	48
§7.	VERBS, Beginner, Intermediate, and Advanced Levels		49
7.1	Agreement		49
7.2	Past Participle		52
7.3	Types		54
	7.3–1	Helping Verbs (Auxiliary Verbs) *avoir* and *être*	54

	7.3–2 Transitive Verbs	59
	7.3–3 Intransitive Verbs	60
7.4	Present Participle	60
7.5	Verbs and Prepositions	62
7.6	Complete Conjugation of an *avoir* Verb	74
7.7	Complete Conjugation of an *être* Verb	78
7.8	Tenses and Moods	81

Beginner Level

	7.8–1 Present Indicative Tense	81
	7.8–2 Imperfect Indicative Tense	83
	7.8–3 Simple Past Tense	84
	7.8–4 Future Tense	85
	7.8–5 Conditional Present Tense	86

Intermediate Level

	7.8–6 Present Subjunctive Tense	87
	7.8–7 Imperfect Subjunctive Tense	88
	7.8–8 Past Indefinite Tense (Passé Composé)	89
	7.8–9 Pluperfect Tense	89

Advanced Level

	7.8–10 Past Anterior Tense	90
	7.8–11 Future Perfect Tense	91
	7.8–12 Conditional Perfect Tense	92
	7.8–13 Past Subjunctive Tense	92
	7.8–14 Pluperfect Subjunctive Tense	93
	7.8–15 Imperative Mood	93

Intermediate and Advanced Levels

7.9	Passive Voice	94
7.10	*Si* Clause: A Summary	95
7.11	Special Uses of Common Verbs	96
7.12	Other Verbs with Special Meanings	102

7.13 Infinitives 103
7.14 Causative (Causal) *Faire* 104
7.15 Subjunctive 105
7.16 Summary of Tenses and Moods 110
7.17 Spelling Irregularities of Some
Common Verbs (Orthographical Changes) 110
7.18 Basic Negations of Verbs 123
7.19 Four Conjugated Verbs 124
§8. ADVERBS 130
Definition 130
8.1 Formation 130
8.2 Position 131
8.3 Types 131
8.3–1 Interrogative Adverbs 131
8.3–2 Adverbs of Quantity 132
8.3–3 Comparative and Superlative
Adverbs 132
8.4 *Oui* and *Si* 133
§9. PREPOSITIONS—SPECIAL USES 134
9.1 *Dans* and *En* + a Length of Time 134
9.2 *Envers* and *Vers* 134
9.3 *Pendant* 135
§10. CONJUNCTIONS 136
10.1 Definition 136
10.2 Basic Conjunctions 136

Special Topics

§11. ORDER OF ELEMENTS IN FRENCH
SENTENCES 139
11.1 Review of Negative Constructions 139
11.2 Declarative Sentence with a Verb in a
Simple Tense 139

11.3 Declarative Sentence with a Verb in a
Compound Tense 140
11.4 Affirmative Imperative Sentence 140
11.5 Negative Imperative Sentence 141
§12. IDIOMS AND IDIOMATIC EXPRESSIONS 142
12.1 Special Uses 142
12.2 Basic Expressions,
Beginner and Intermediate Levels 145
§13. DATES, DAYS, MONTHS, SEASONS 162
13.1 Dates 162
13.2 Days 162
13.3 Months 163
13.4 Seasons 163
§14. TELLING TIME 164
14.1 Time Expressions You Ought to Know 164
14.2 "Official" Time Expressions 165
§15. TALKING ABOUT THE WEATHER 167
§16. NUMBERS 169
§17. SYNONYMS 174
§18. ANTONYMS 179
§19. COGNATES 185
§20. TRICKY WORDS 187
§21. HOW TO ASK A QUESTION 189
**§22. DEFINITIONS OF BASIC GRAMMATICAL
TERMS WITH EXAMPLES IN
FRENCH AND ENGLISH** 191

French-English Vocabulary 224

Index 233

About the Authors

Dr. Christopher Kendris has worked as an interpreter and translator of French for the U.S. State Department at the American Embassy in Paris. He earned his B.S. in the School of General Studies and his M.S. in the School of Library Service, both at Columbia University in the City of New York, where he held a New York State Scholarship. He earned his M.A. and Ph.D. at Northwestern University in Evanston, Illinois, where he held a teaching assistantship and tutorial fellowship for four years. He also earned two diplomas with *Mention très Honorable* at the Université de Paris (en Sorbonne), Faculté des Lettres, École Supérieure de Préparation et de Perfectionnement des Professeurs de Français à l'Étranger, and at the Institut de Phonétique, Paris. His highly esteemed mentor was Dr. Bernard Weinberg, a teacher, author, scholar, friend, and professor of romance languages and literatures at the University of Chicago in Chicago, Illinois, and Northwestern University in Evanston, Illinois.

In 1986, Dr. Kendris was one of ninety-five teachers in the United States to be awarded a Rockefeller Foundation Fellowship for Teachers of Foreign Languages in American High Schools. He has had forty years of teaching experience. Dr. Kendris has taught French and Spanish at the University of Chicago as a visiting summer lecturer, as well as at Colby College, Duke University, Rutgers (the State University of New Jersey), the State University of New York at Albany, the Albany Academy, the Schenectady School District, and the Schenectady County Community College in New York. He was Chairman of the Department of Foreign Languages at

Farmingdale High School in Farmingdale, New York, where he was also a teacher of all levels of French and Spanish, and he prepared students for the New York State French and Spanish Regents exams, SAT exams, and AP tests. Dr. Kendris is the author of thirty-two secondary school and college books, workbooks, and other language guides of French and Spanish, some of which have been best sellers since 1970 all over the world, and all of which have been published by Barron's Educational Series. He also worked as a cataloger of books at the U.S. Library of Congress in Washington, D.C., in the 1970s. Dr. Kendris is listed in *Contemporary Authors* and the *Directory of American Scholars.*

Dr. Theodore Kendris earned his B.A. in modern languages at Union College in Schenectady, New York, where he received the Thomas J. Judson Memorial Award for modern language study. He went on to earn his M.A. in French language and literature at Northwestern University in Evanston, Illinois, where he was a teaching assistant and senior teaching fellow. He earned his Ph.D. in French literature at l'Université Laval in Quebec City, where he studied the Middle Ages and Renaissance. While at Université Laval, he taught French writing skills as *chargé de cours* in the French as a Second Language program, and in 1997 he was awarded a doctoral scholarship by the Fondation de l'Université Laval. Dr. Kendris has also taught in the Department of English and Foreign Languages at the University of St. Francis in Joliet, Illinois, as well as at the Hazleton campus of Penn State University.

Dr. Kendris is the author of *Inglés completo: Repaso integral de gramática inglesa para hispanohablantes,* published by Barron's in 2008. He is also the coauthor of several language guides, including *Pronounce It Perfectly in French, French Vocabulary, E-Z French, 501 Spanish Verbs, Seventh Edition,* and *501 French Verbs, Sixth Edition,* also published by Barron's.

How to Use This Book

In the chapters that follow, a numerical decimal system has been used with the symbol § in front of it. This was done so that you may find quickly and easily the reference to a particular point in basic French grammar when you use the index. For example, if you look up the entry "adjectives" in the index, you will find the reference given as **§5**. Sometimes additional § reference numbers are given when the entry you consult is mentioned in other areas in the chapter §. For example, in §5.3, there is an explanation of how to decide whether an adjective belongs before or after the noun that it modifies. The index also includes some key French words, for example, avoir and être, with § references also given to them.

Preface

This book is part of a series of handy basic grammar reference guides. It is designed for students, businesspeople, and others who want to "brush up" their knowledge of basic French grammar. Definitions and explanations are concise and clear. Plenty of examples use and reuse a core of basic vocabulary.

This pocket-size book contains essential French grammar that is normally in the curriculum of beginning, intermediate, and advanced language programs. It is a reference grammar review book of all three levels. We hope you enjoy, in particular, our section on what preposition goes with what verb, found on pages 62–74.

The complete grammar review consists of three parts: the Basics, the Parts of Speech, and Special Topics, all of which are outlined in the table of contents.

Here and there we offer some tips to help you remember certain aspects of French grammar and vocabulary. For example, if you cannot remember whether the French word for twenty (vingt) is spelled *ng* or *gn*, remember it this way:

Tip	*VI* $\boxed{N}$ *GT*
	TWE $\boxed{N}$ TY

Mnemonic tips are very useful in learning and remembering. Students learn and remember in different ways. What works for you may not work for someone else. You must think of ways to help yourself remember. If you think of a way that is helpful, let it work for you. One student in a Spanish class, for example, told Dr. C. Kendris that she finally figured out a way to remember the meaning of the Spanish verb *buscar* / to look for. She said, "I'm looking for a bus or a car." How many mnemonic tips can you make up in French? Try it. It's fun! Here are a few more: If someone asks you, "What are the five major Romance Languages?" are you going to say you don't know? Remember **FRIPS**:

Tip	**F**rench
	Romanian
	Italian
	Portuguese
	Spanish

To remember that there are only four nasal vowels in French, hang on to this catchy phrase because each word contains one of the four nasal vowels:

Tip	*un bon vin blanc* / a good white wine

If you keep pronouncing *un œuf* / an egg incorrectly, say this out loud:

Tip	Do you want one egg? Two eggs?
	One egg is enough!
	One egg is *un œuf*!

The sound of the English word "enough" is very close to the sound of the French word *un œuf*.

There are more mnemonic tips throughout this book. If we have omitted anything you think is important, if you spot any misprints, or if you have any suggestions for the improvement of the next edition, please write to us, care of the publisher.

This edition of *French Grammar* offers an important feature—color as an aid to learning. Throughout this book, the intricacies of the French language are made clearer by color highlights. We hope you will find that color makes every section of this book easier to understand and use effectively.

Whatever facilitates learning enhances the ability to use what is learned.

Dr. C. Kendris would like to thank Françoise Lapouille, his friend and colleague, who was born and educated in France and has been a teacher of French for many years. She holds the degree of *Licence ès Lettres* from the Université de Paris (La Sorbonne). We sincerely appreciate her helpful suggestions while reading the original manuscript of this book to make sure that the French contained in it is *juste et comme il faut*, correct and as it should be.

Christopher Kendris
B.S., M.S., M.A., Ph.D.

Theodore Kendris
B.A., M.A., Ph.D.

The Basics, Beginner Level

§1.

Guide to Pronouncing French Sounds

English words given here contain sounds that only approximate French sounds.

PURE VOWEL SOUNDS	
Pronounced as in the	
French word	**English word**
la	lolly, Tom
pas	ah!
été	ate
ère, tête	egg
ici	see
hôtel	over
donne	bun, done
ou	too
leur	urgent (approx. sound)
deux	pudding (approx. sound)
tu	cute (approx. sound)
le	ago (approx. sound)

NASAL VOWEL SOUNDS

(English sounds are approximate.)

un	**un**guent, su**ng**
bon	so**ng**
vin	sa**ng**
blanc	thro**ng**

SEMICONSONANT SOUNDS

(Also called semivowels)

oui	**w**est
huit	**y**ou **ea**t (approx. sound)
fille	**y**es, see **y**a later

CONSONANT SOUNDS

Pronounced as in the

French word	English word
bonne	**b**un
dans	**d**og
fou	**f**irst, **ph**armacy
garçon	**g**o
je	mea**s**ure
chose	**sh**ake
café, qui	**c**ap, **k**ennel
le	**l**et
mette	**m**et
nette	**n**et
montagne	can**y**on, on**i**on, un**i**on
camping	camp**ing**, sleep**ing**
père	**p**ear
rose	**r**ose (approx. sound; the French sound is pronounced further back in the throat.)

si	**s**ee
te	**l**ot
vous	**v**ine
zèbre	**z**ebra
ça	**s**orry

- If you can, give equal stress to all syllables in a French word; do not raise your voice on any particular syllable.
- If you can't give equal stress to all syllables in a French word, then raise your voice slightly on the last syllable.

  Examples:
  chapeau (shah-PO), *magazine* (mah-gah-ZEEN), *perspicacité* (per-spee-kah-see-TAY)

- Do not pronounce the last letter of a French word if it is a consonant.

  Examples:
  beaucoup (bo-KOO), *aéroport* (ah-air-o-POR)

Some common exceptions: *parc* (pARK), *chef* (shEFF), *avec* (ah-VEK). If you're not sure, don't pronounce the last consonant at all.

 If you don't know which is *accent aigu* (acute) (*é*) and which is *accent grave* (*è*), remember that the patient died of acute appendicitis (*é*) and ended up in the grave (*è*).

Pronunciation of Orthographically Changing Verb Forms (Changes in Spelling)

1. Normally, in a French word the consonant **c** in front of **a**, **o**, or **u** is pronounced as *k* (cap, cop, cup). Verbs ending in **-cer** change **c** to **ç** (**c cédille**) in front of **a** or **o** in order to keep the *s* sound of the infinitive. Example: **commencer/je commençais**

2. Normally, in a French word the consonant **g** in front of **a**, **o**, or **u** is pronounced hard (game, go, gum). Verbs ending in **-ger** add **e** after **g** in front of **a** or **o** in order to keep the soft sound of **g** (as in **je**) of the infinitive. Example: **manger/nous mangeons**.

3. Verbs ending in **-eler** or **-eter** change as follows:
   (a) Single **l** or single **t** doubles in front of a syllable containing mute **e** because the stress is on that syllable. Examples: **appeler/j'appelle; jeter/je jette**
   (b) Mute **e** changes to **è** when in front of a syllable that contains mute **e** because the stress is on that syllable. Examples: **acheter/j'achète; geler/je gèle**

§2.
Capitalization, Punctuation Marks, and Word Division

§2.1 CAPITALIZATION

Generally speaking, French capitalization is similar to English in that you must capitalize the first letter of a sentence as well as the names of people and places.

Lundi prochain, Marie va faire un voyage en Afrique. Next Monday, Mary is going to take a trip to Africa.

When they are found elsewhere in a sentence, you must not capitalize days of the week, months of the year, languages, adjectives of nationality, and religions.

> *dimanche, lundi, mardi, etc.; janvier, février, mars, etc.; français, espagnol, anglais, etc.; Antonio est italien, María es espagnole; Pierre est français; Jacques est catholique.*

Nouns of nationality are capitalized.

un Américain / an American (male);
une Française / a French woman.

§2.2 PUNCTUATION MARKS

The basic punctuation marks in French are:

> *le point* / period   .
> *point virgule* / semicolon   ;
> *la virgule* / comma   ,
> *l'apostrophe (f)* / apostrophe   '
> *deux points* / colon   :
> *les parenthèses (f)* / parentheses   ( )
> *les guillemets (m)* / quotation marks   " "
> *le point d'interrogation* / question mark   ?
> *les points de suspension* / ellipses points   . . .

5

§2.3   WORD DIVISION

It is good to know how to divide a word into syllables (not only in French but also in English) because it helps you pronounce and spell the word correctly.

Basic Rules

- A syllable must contain a vowel, but it may contain only one vowel and no consonant.

  é / cole (*école* / school)

- When you are dealing with single separate consonants, each consonant remains with the vowel that follows it.

  beau / coup (*beaucoup* / many, much)

- When two consonants come together, they are separated; the first remains with the preceding syllable and the second remains with the following syllable.

  im / por / tant (*important*)

But if the second of the two consonants that come together is *l* or *r*, do not separate them:

  a / près (*après* / after); *im / meu / ble* (*immeuble* / building, apartment building)

- When three consonants come together, the first two remain with the preceding vowel and the third remains with the vowel that follows it.

  ins / ti / tut (*institut*)

But if the third of the three consonants is *l* or *r*, do not separate that third consonant from the second; it remains with the second consonant.

  com / pren / dre (*comprendre* / to understand)

Vowels

- Two vowels together are generally separated if they are strong vowels *(a, e, o)*.

  a / é / ro / port (*aéroport* / airport)

But if you are dealing with a weak vowel *(i, u)*, it ordinarily remains in the same syllable with its neighboring vowel, especially if that other vowel is a strong vowel.

huî / tre (*huître* / oyster)

The Parts of Speech

§3.

Articles, Beginner Level

§3.1   DEFINITE ARTICLE

The definite article in French has four forms, and they all mean "the":

Gender	Singular	Plural
Masculine	*le, l'*	*les*
Feminine	*la, l'*	*les*

Singular	Plural
le garçon / the boy	*les garçons* / the boys
l'arbre (m) / the tree	*les arbres* / the trees
la jeune fille / the girl	*les jeunes filles* / the girls
l'école / the school	*les écoles* / the schools

Definite Article Used

WITH NOUNS

- Before each noun even when more than one noun is stated.

    J'ai le livre et le cahier. / I have the book and notebook.

- When you make a general statement.

    J'aime le lait. / I like milk.
    J'aime l'été. / I like summer.

- With a noun of weight or measure to express "a," "an," "per."

    dix euros le kilo / ten euros per kilo
    vingt euros la douzaine / twenty euros a dozen

- Before a noun indicating a profession, rank, or title followed by the name of the person.

    Le professeur Poulin est absent aujourd'hui. / Professor Poulin is absent today.

- With the name of a language.

    J'étudie le français. / I'm studying French.

    EXCEPTION: Do *not* use the definite article when the name of a language directly follows a form of the verb *parler*.

    Je parle français et russe. / I speak French and Russian.

- With the days of the week to indicate an action that is habitually repeated.

    Le samedi je vais au cinéma. / On Saturdays I go to the movies.

But when you want to indicate a *particular* day, do not use the definite article.

    Samedi je vais au cinéma. / Saturday I am going to the movies. (understood: this Saturday)

With parts of the body or articles of clothing if the possessor is clearly stated.

    Luigi, qui est italien, a les cheveux noirs. / Luigi, who is Italian, has black hair.

With family names in the plural, in which case the spelling of the family name does not change.

> *Nous allons chez les Durand.* / We're going to the Durands.

WITH PREPOSITIONS

When the prepositions *à* and *de* come before the definite article, it contracts as follows:

Preposition		Article		Contraction
à	+	le	>	*au*
	+	les	>	*aux*
de	+	le	>	*du*
	+	les	>	*des*

But there is *no* change with *l'* or *la*.

> *Je vais à l'aéroport.* / I'm going to the airport.
> *Je vais à la bibliothèque.* / I'm going to the library.
> *Je viens de l'aéroport.* / I'm coming from the airport.
> *Je viens de la bibliothèque.* / I'm coming from the library.

With the preposition *à* (which combines to form *au* or *aux*) in front of the name of a country that is masculine.

> *Nous allons au Canada.* / We're going to Canada.
> *Janine vient aux États-Unis.* / Janine is coming to the United States.

With the preposition *de* (which combines to form *du* or *des*) before the name of a country that is masculine.

> *du Portugal* / from Portugal
> *des Etats-Unis* / from the United States

With the preposition *de* + a common noun to indicate possession.

le livre du garçon / the boy's book
les livres des garçons / the boys' books
la robe de la jeune fille / the girl's dress
les poupées des petites filles / the little girls' dolls

WITH CERTAIN EXPRESSIONS

• Indicating segments of the day.

l'après-midi / in the afternoon; *le matin* / in the morning;
le soir / in the evening

• Common expressions.

à l'école / to school, in school; *à la maison* / at home
la semaine dernière / last week; *l'année dernière* / last year
la plupart de / most of
la plupart des jeunes filles / most of the girls

• As a partitive in the affirmative.

J'ai du café. / I have (some) coffee.
Tu as de l'argent. / You have (some) money.
Il a des amis. / He has friends.

Definite Article Not Used

However, the definite article is *not* used when the partitive is in the negative or when the definite article is used with an adjective.

Je n'ai pas de café. / I haven't any coffee.
Tu n'as pas d'argent. / You haven't any money.
Il a de bons amis. / He has some good friends.

Do not use the definite article:

In direct address: *Bonjour, docteur Leduc.*
After the preposition *en: Nous écrivons en français.*
Exceptions:

en l'air / in the air; *en l'absence de* / in the absence of;
en l'honneur de / in honor of

After the preposition *de* in an adjective phrase: *J'aime mon livre de français.*

With a feminine country and continents when you use
en / at, to or *de* / of, from.

> *Je vais en France, en Angleterre, en Allemagne, en Australie, en
> Asie, et en Amérique.*
> *Paul vient de France, les Armstrong viennent d'Australie et Hilda
> vient d'Allemagne.* '

With most cities: *à Paris, à New York; de Londres, de
Montréal, de Sydney.*

With a noun in apposition: *Paul, fils du professeur Leblanc, est
très aimable.*

With titles of monarchs.

> *Louis Seize (Louis XVI)* / Louis the Sixteenth

With the preposition *sans* or with the construction *ne . . .
ni . . . ni . . . :*

> *Je n'ai ni papier ni stylo.* / I have neither paper nor pen.
> *Il est parti sans argent.* / He left without money.

With certain expressions of quantity that take *de: beaucoup
de, trop de, combien de, peu de, plus de, assez de*

> *Marie a beaucoup d'amis.* / Marie has a lot of (many) friends.

With the preposition *avec* when the noun after it is abstract:

> *Jean-Luc parle avec enthousiasme.*

§3.2   INDEFINITE ARTICLE

The forms of the indefinite article are:

Singular
J'ai **un** *frère.* / I have a brother.
J'ai **une** *sœur.* / I have a sister.

Plural
J'ai **des** *frères.* / I have brothers.
J'ai **des** *sœurs.* / I have sisters.

The indefinite article is used:

- When you want to say "a" or "an." It is also used as a numeral to mean "one":

    un livre / a book or one book
    une orange / an orange or one orange

- In front of each noun in a series:

    J'ai un cahier, un crayon et une gomme. / I have a notebook, pencil, and eraser.

- With *C'est* or *Ce sont* with or without an adjective:

    C'est un docteur. / He's a doctor.
    C'est un mauvais docteur. / He's a bad doctor.
    Ce sont des étudiants. / They are students.

The indefinite article is *not* used:

- With *cent* and *mille:*

    J'ai cent dollars. / I have a hundred dollars.
    J'ai mille dollars. / I have a thousand dollars.

- With *il est, ils sont, elle est, elles sont* + an unmodified noun of nationality, profession, or religion:

    Elle est professeur. / She is a professor.
    Il est catholique. / He is (a) Catholic.

When you use *quel* in an exclamation:

    Quelle femme! / What a woman!
    Quel homme! / What a man!

With negations, particularly with the verb *avoir*:

    Avez-vous un livre? Non, je n'ai pas de livre. / Have you a book? No, I don't have a book (any book).

§3.3   PARTITIVE

The partitive denotes a *part* of a whole; in other words, some. In English, we express the partitive by saying "some" or "any" in front of the noun. Use the following forms in front of the noun:

Masculine singular: *du* or *de l'*
Feminine singular: *de la* or *de l'*
Masculine or feminine plural: *des*

| Tip | If the thing you are talking about can be counted individually, you should not use the partitive. You should use the indefinite article: **J'ai des bonbons.** / I have some candy. (You can eat a single **bonbon**.) |

Simple Affirmative

J'ai **du** *café.* / I have some coffee.
J'ai **de la** *viande.* / I have some meat.
J'ai **de l'***eau.* / I have some water.

There can be a partitive in the plural as long as you are not, in fact, talking about something countable.

Je mange **des** *pâtes.* / I am eating pasta.

Simple Negative

Je **n'***ai* **pas de** *café.* / I don't have any coffee.
Je **n'***ai* **pas de** *viande.* / I don't have any meat.
Je **n'***ai* **pas d'***eau.* / I don't have any water.
Je **n'***ai* **pas d'***épinards.* / I don't have any spinach.
Je **n'***ai* **pas de** *pâtes.* / I don't have any pasta.

With an Adjective

J'ai **de jolis** *chapeaux.* / I have some pretty hats.
J'ai **de jolies** *robes.* / I have some pretty dresses.

Note the following:

- When the noun is preceded by an adverb or noun of quantity or measure, use *de*, as in *J'ai beaucoup de choses.* / I have many things.
- When the noun is modified by another noun, use *de*, as in *une école de danse* / a school of dance.
- The partitive is not used with *sans* or *ne . . . ni . . . ni.*

   Example:
   J'ai quitté la maison sans argent. / I left the house without any money.

- Use *quelques* and not the partitive when by "some" you mean "a few," in other words, "not many."

   Examples:
   J'ai quelques amis. / I have a few (some) friends.
   J'ai quelques bonbons. / I have a few (some) candies.

- When the negated verb is *ne . . . que* / only, the partitive consists of *de* plus the definite article.

   Examples:
   Elle ne lit que des livres. / She reads only books.
   Elle ne mange que des bonbons. / She eats only candy.

- The partitive must be repeated before each noun.

   Example:
   Ici on vend du papier, de l'encre et des cahiers. / Here they sell paper, ink, and notebooks.

 Tip When you are ordering food, it is possible to use an indefinite article to refer to the serving.
Un café, s'il vous plaît. / A (cup of) coffee, please.

§4.
Nouns, Beginner Level

§4.1 GENDER

A *noun* is a word that refers to a person, place, thing, or quality. Nouns are either masculine or feminine and require the article *le, la, l'*, or *les*. The gender of many nouns that refer to persons or animals is obvious. However, nouns that refer to some animals are not always evident. (See below.)

Examples

PERSONS	
Masculine	**Feminine**
l'homme / the man	*la femme* / the woman
le garçon / the boy	*la jeune fille* / the girl
l'oncle / the uncle	*la tante* / the aunt

ANIMALS	
Masculine	**Feminine**
le taureau / the bull	*la vache* / the cow
le coq / the rooster	*la poule* / the hen
le chat / the cat	*la chatte* / the cat

Sometimes the gender of a noun does not match the gender of the animal to which it refers. Here are a few examples:

une chèvre / a goat
un crocodile / a crocodile
une girafe / a giraffe
une sauterelle / a grasshopper
une souris / a mouse

- The gender of nouns referring to anything other than persons or animals must be learned with the noun.

Examples

Gender	Noun Endings	Examples
Masculine	*-age or -âge*	*l'âge* / age
		le fromage / cheese
	-ment	*le logement* / lodging
		le médicament / medicine (you take)
	-eau	*le chapeau* / hat
		le gâteau / cake
Feminine	*-ance*	*la circonstance* / circumstance
		la chance / chance, luck
	-ence	*l'apparence* / appearance
		la science / science
	-tion	*l'attention* / attention
		la notion / idea, notion
	-ette	*la fourchette* / fork
		la serviette / napkin
		la sucette / lollipop

Special Cases

Some nouns have one meaning when masculine, another meaning when feminine:

Masculine	**Feminine**
le critique / critic	*la critique* / criticism
le livre / book	*la livre* / pound
le manche / handle	*la manche* / sleeve
le poêle / wood stove	*la poêle* / frying pan
le poste / job	*la poste* / mail, post office
le somme / nap	*la somme* / sum total
le tour / turn, tour	*la tour* / tower
le vase / vase	*la vase* / mud
le voile / veil	*la voile* / sail

Some nouns are the same for both:

Masculine	**Feminine**
un élève / pupil (boy)	*une élève* / pupil (girl)
un enfant / child (boy)	*une enfant* / child (girl)

Some nouns add *-e* to the masculine to form the feminine:

Masculine	**Feminine**
un cousin / cousin	*une cousine* / cousin
un ami / friend	*une amie* / friend

Some nouns change the *-eur* masculine ending to *-euse* for feminine:

Masculine	**Feminine**
un vendeur / salesman	*une vendeuse* / saleswoman
un menteur / liar	*une menteuse* / liar

Some masculine *-teur* nouns change to *-trice* in the feminine:

un acteur / actor	*une actrice*
un aviateur / aviator	*une aviatrice*
un spectateur / spectator	*une spectatrice*

In your studies, if you are not sure of the feminine form of a French noun or adjective in the singular or plural, you must get into the habit of looking up words in a dictionary.

§4.2 PLURAL OF NOUNS—THE BASICS

Add *-s* to the singular:

Singular	Plural
le livre / the book	*les livres* / the books
la maison / the house	*les maisons* / the houses
l'étudiant / the student	*les étudiants* / the students

If a noun ends in *-s, -x,* or *-z* in the singular, leave it alone:

Singular	Plural
le bras / the arm	*les bras* / the arms
la voix / the voice	*les voix* / the voices
le nez / the nose	*les nez* / the noses

If a noun ends in *-al* in the singular, change *-al* to *-aux:*

Singular
le journal / the newspaper

Plural
les journaux / the newspapers

If a noun ends in *-eu* or *-eau* in the singular, add *-x:*

Singular
le feu / the fire
le bureau / the office, the desk

Plural
les feux / the fires
les bureaux / the offices, the desks

Common irregular nouns

Singular	Plural
le ciel / the sky	*les cieux* / the skies
l'œil / the eye	*les yeux* / the eyes

§5.

Adjectives, Beginner Level

§5.1 FORMATION

Feminine Singular

The feminine singular of an adjective is normally formed by adding *-e* to the masculine singular.

> **Examples:**
> *joli—jolie* / pretty   *présent—présente* / present
> *grand—grande* / tall

If a masculine singular adjective already ends in *-e*, the feminine singular is the same form.

> **Examples:**
> *aimable* / kind   *énorme* / huge   *faible* / weak

Some feminine singular forms are irregular. If a masculine singular adjective ends in *-c*, change it to *-que* for the feminine; *-er* to *-ère*; *-f* to *-ve*; *-g* to *-gue*; and *-x* to *-se*.

> **Examples:**
> *public—publique* / public   *long—longue* / long
> *premier—première* / first   *heureux—heureuse* / happy
> *actif—active* / active

Some masculine singular adjectives double the final consonant before adding *-e* to form the feminine.

> **Examples:**
> *ancien—ancienne* / old   *cruel—cruelle* / cruel
> *bas—basse* / low   *gentil—gentille* / kind, nice
> *bon—bonne* / good   *sot—sotte* / foolish
> *pareil—pareille* / similar   *épais—épaisse* / thick

- The following feminine singular adjectives are formed from the irregular masculine singular forms:

Masculine Singular Before a Masculine Singular Noun Beginning with a Consonant	Irregular Masculine Singular Before a Masculine Singular Noun Beginning with a Vowel or Silent *H*
beau / beautiful, handsome	*bel ami*
fou / crazy	*fol ami*
nouveau / new	*nouvel hôtel*
vieux / old	*vieil ami*

Feminine Singular
belle amie
folle amie
nouvelle amie
vieille amie

Tip *La vieille dame a passé la veille de Noël avec son vieil ami dans un vieux cabaret.* / The old lady spent Christmas Eve with her old friend in an old cabaret.

• Some common masculine singular adjectives have irregular forms in the feminine singular. These do not fall into any particular category like those above.

Examples:

blanc—blanche / white
complet—complète / complete
doux—douce / soft, smooth, sweet
faux—fausse / false
favori—favorite / favorite
frais—fraîche / fresh
sec—sèche / dry

Plural

- The plural is normally formed by adding *-s* to the masculine or feminine singular.

  Examples:
  bon—bons; bonne—bonnes / good   *joli—jolis; jolie—jolies* / pretty

- If the masculine singular already ends in *-s* or *-x*, it remains the same in the masculine plural.

  Examples:
  gris—gris /gray   *heureux—heureux* / happy

- If a masculine singular adjective ends in *-al*, it changes to *-aux* (with some exceptions).

  Examples:
  égal—égaux / equal   *principal—principaux* / principal
  Exception: *fatal—fatals* / fatal

- If a masculine singular adjective ends in *-eau*, it changes to *-eaux*.

  Examples:
  nouveau—nouveaux / new   *beau—beaux* / beautiful, handsome

§5.2   AGREEMENT

An adjective agrees in gender (feminine or masculine) and number (singular or plural) with the noun or pronoun it modifies. If the verb is a form of *être* (to be), an agreement is made on the adjective with the subject.

Examples:
Alexandre et Théodore sont beaux et intelligents. / Alexander and
  Theodore are handsome and smart.
Yolande est belle. / Yolande is beautiful.
Janine et Monique sont belles. / Janine and Monique are beautiful.
Hélène et Simone sont actives. / Helene and Simone are active.
Anne est jolie. / Anne is pretty.
C'est un bel arbre. / It is a beautiful tree.
Ils sont amusants. / They are amusing.

Chaque garçon est présent. / Every boy is here (present).
Chaque jeune fille est présente. / Every girl is here (present).
Valentine est absente. / Valentine is absent.

Note that you must use the masculine plural form of the adjective when it modifies nouns, proper nouns, or pronouns of mixed gender: *Daniel et Danielle sont américains.* / Daniel and Danielle are American.

§5.3 POSITION

- In French, most descriptive adjectives are placed after the noun; e.g., colors, nationality, religion: *une robe blanche* / a white dress, *un fromage français* / a French cheese, *une femme catholique* / a Catholic woman
- Here are some examples of common short adjectives that are generally placed in front of the noun:

  un autre livre / another book, *un bel arbre* / a beautiful tree, *un beau cadeau* / a beautiful gift, *un bon dîner* / a good dinner, *chaque jour* / each day, *un gros livre* / a big book, *une jeune dame* / a young lady, *une jolie maison* / a pretty house, *une petite table* / a small table, *plusieurs amis* / several friends, *un vieil homme* / an old man, *le premier rang* / the first row, *quelques bonbons* / some candy, *un tel garçon* / such a boy, *toute la journée* / all day.

- Some adjectives change in meaning, depending on whether the adjective is in front of the noun or after it. The most common are:

  la semaine dernière / last week

  ma robe propre / my clean dress

  une femme brave / a brave woman

  le même moment / the same moment

  un livre cher / an expensive book

  la dernière semaine / the last (final) week

  ma propre robe / my own dress

  une brave femme / a fine woman

  le moment même / the very moment

  un cher ami / a dear friend

§5.4   TYPES

§5.4–1   Descriptive

A descriptive adjective is a word that describes a noun or pronoun: *une belle maison* / a beautiful house, *un beau livre* / a beautiful book, *un bel arbre* / a beautiful tree, *une jolie femme* / a pretty woman, *un chapeau gris* / a gray hat, *une jupe bleue* / a blue skirt, *une femme brave* / a brave woman.

> *Elle est grande.* / She is tall.

§5.4–2   Demonstrative

A demonstrative adjective is used to point out something or someone.

Gender	Singular	Plural
Masculine	*ce, cet* / this, that	*ces* / these, those
Feminine	*cette* / this, that	*ces* / these, those

Examples:
Ce garçon est beau. / This boy is handsome.
Cet arbre est beau. / This tree is beautiful.
Cette femme est belle. / This woman is beautiful.
Ces hommes sont beaux. / These men are handsome.
Ces livres sont beaux. / These books are beautiful.
Ces dames sont belles. / These ladies are beautiful.

 Tip   If you wish to make a contrast between "this" and "that" or "these" and "those," add *-ci* this, these or *-là* that, those to the noun with a hyphen.

Ce garçon-ci est plus fort que ce garçon-là. / This boy is stronger than that boy.

The form *cet* is used in front of a masculine singular noun or adjective beginning with a vowel or silent *h: cet arbre, cet homme.*

If there is more than one noun, a demonstrative adjective must be used in front of each noun: *cette dame et ce monsieur.*

§5.4–3 Interrogative

The adjective *quel* is generally regarded as interrogative because it is frequently used in a question. Its forms are *quel, quelle, quels, quelles.* Note that in English the translation is *which* or *what.*

Examples:
Quel livre voulez-vous? / Which book do you want?
Quel est votre nom? / What is your name?
Quelle heure est-il? / What time is it?
Quelle est votre adresse? / What is your address?
Quels sont les mois de l'année? / What are the months of the year?
Quelles sont les saisons? / What are the seasons?

The adjective *quel* is also used in exclamations. Note that the indefinite article *un (une)* is not used in this case.

Examples:
Quel garçon! / What a boy!
Quelle jeune fille! / What a girl!

§5.4–4 Possessive

MASCULINE	
Singular	**Plural**
mon livre / my book	*mes livres* / my books
ton stylo / your pen	*tes stylos* / your pens
son ballon / his (her, its) balloon	*ses ballons* / his (her, its) balloons
notre parapluie / our umbrella	*nos parapluies* / our umbrellas
votre sandwich / your sandwich	*vos sandwichs* / your sandwiches
leur gâteau / their cake	*leurs gâteaux* / their cakes

FEMININE	
Singular	**Plural**
ma robe / my dress	*mes robes* / my dresses
ta jaquette / your jacket	*tes jaquettes* / your jackets
sa balle / his (her, its) ball	*ses balles* / his (her, its) balls
notre maison / our house	*nos maisons* / our houses
votre voiture / your car	*vos voitures* / your cars
leur sœur / their sister	*leurs sœurs* / their sisters

- A possessive adjective agrees in gender and number with the noun it modifies.
- *Notre, votre*, and *leur* do not agree with the gender of the noun in the singular. They are all the same, whether in front of a masculine or feminine singular noun.
- Possessive adjectives do not agree with the gender of the noun in the plural. They are all the same, whether in front of a masculine or feminine plural noun: *mes, tes, ses, nos, vos, leurs.*
- Be aware of *mon (ma), ton (ta), son (sa)*: In front of a feminine singular noun beginning with a vowel or silent *h*, the masculine singular forms are used: *mon, ton, son*—not *ma, ta, sa.*

mon adresse / my address
ton opinion / your opinion
son amie / his (or her) friend
mon habitude / my habit (custom)

Tip	• Since *son, sa*, and *ses* can mean "his" or "her," you may add *à lui* or *à elle* to make the meaning clear.

> *sa maison à lui* / his house
> *sa maison à elle* / her house
> *son livre à lui* / his book
> *son livre à elle* / her book
> *ses livres à lui* / his books
> *ses livres à elle* / her books

Tip
* If there is more than one noun, a possessive adjective must be used in front of each noun: *ma mère et mon père, mon livre et mon cahier.*

Possessive Adjectives with Parts of the Body and Clothing

* When using the verb *avoir*, the definite article is normally used with parts of the body, **not** the possessive adjective.

    Henri a les mains sales. / Henry has dirty hands.
    Simone a les cheveux roux. / Simone has red hair.

* When using a reflexive verb, the definite article is normally used, **not** the possessive adjective.

    Paulette s'est lavé les cheveux. / Paulette washed her hair.

* The *definite article* is used instead of the possessive adjective when referring to parts of the body or clothing if it is clear who the possessor is.

    Henri tient le livre dans la main. / Henry is holding the book in his hand.

§5.4–5 Comparative and Superlative

Comparative

Of the same degree: *aussi . . . que* / as . . . as
Of a lesser degree: *moins . . . que* / less . . . than
Of a higher degree: *plus . . . que* / more . . . than

Janine est aussi grande que Monique. / Janine is as tall as Monique.
Monique est moins intelligente que Janine. / Monique is less
  intelligent than Janine.
Janine est plus jolie que Monique. / Janine is prettier than Monique.

- *Aussi . . . que* often becomes *si . . . que* in a negative sentence.

  Robert n'est pas si grand que Joseph. / Robert is not as tall as
    Joseph.

  This change is not always made. You may also hear or read:
    Robert n'est pas **aussi** grand que Joseph.

The comparative and superlative forms of the adjective "bad"
are irregular. To say "worse" you can say *pire* or *plus
mauvais(e)*. "The worst" is *le/la pire* or *le/la plus mauvais(e)*.
It is more proper to say *pire* or *le/la pire*, but *plus mauvais,
plus mauvaise, le plus mauvais,* and *la plus mauvaise,* are also
used by native speakers.

  Ce stylo est *mauvais.* / This pen is bad.
  Ce stylo est *plus mauvais* que l'autre. **Or,** Ce stylo est *pire* que
    l'autre. / This pen is worse than the other.
  Ce stylo est *le plus mauvais.* **Or,** Ce stylo est *le pire.* / This pen is
    the worst.
  The plural form is *pires* **Or,** *les pires / les plus mauvais(es).*
  Ces chaussures sont *plus mauvaises* que les autres. **Or,** Ces
    chaussures sont *pires* que les autres. / These shoes are worse
    than the others.
  Ces stylos sont *les plus mauvais.* **Or,** Ces stylos sont *les pires.* /
    These pens are the worst.
  Ces chaussures sont *les plus mauvaises.* **Or,** Ces chaussures
    sont *les pires.* / These shoes are the worst.

- *Plus que* / more than becomes *plus de* + a number.

  Examples:
  Il a plus de cinquante ans. / He is more than fifty years old.
  Je lui ai donné plus de cent dollars. / I gave him (her) more than a
    hundred dollars.

Superlative

- The superlative is formed by placing the appropriate definite
  article *(le, la, les)* in front of the comparative:

Marie est la plus jolie jeune fille de la classe. / Mary is the
   prettiest girl in the class.

- If the adjective normally follows the noun, the definite article
  must be used twice—in front of the noun and in front of the
  superlative:

   Monsieur Hibou fut le président le plus sage de la nation. / Mr.
   Hibou was the wisest president of the nation.

- After a superlative, the preposition *de* (not *dans*) is normally
  used to express "in":

   Pierre est le plus beau garçon de la classe. / Peter is the most
   handsome boy in the class.

- If more than one comparative or superlative is expressed,
  each is repeated:

   Marie est la plus intelligente et la plus sérieuse de l'école. / Mary
   is the most intelligent and most serious in the school.

Tip	*Une devinette* (a riddle) using a superlative:

Quelle est la chose la plus sale de la maison? / What is the
   dirtiest thing in the house?

un balai / a broom

Irregular Comparative and Superlative Adjectives

Adjective (m)	Comparative	Superlative
bon / good	*meilleur* / better	*le meilleur* / (the) best
mauvais / bad	*plus mauvais* / *pire* } worse	*le plus mauvais* / *le pire* } (the) worst
petit / small	*plus petit* / smaller (in size)	*le plus petit* / (the) smallest
	moindre / less (in importance)	*le moindre* / (the) least

§5.4–6   *Meilleur* and *Mieux*

Meilleur is an adjective and must agree in gender and number with the noun or pronoun it modifies.

Example:
> *Cette pomme est bonne, cette pomme-là est meilleure que
> celle-ci et celle-là est la meilleure.* / This apple is good, that
> apple is better than this one, and that one is the best.

Mieux is an adverb and does not change in form.

Example:
> *Marie chante bien, Anne chante mieux que Marie et Claire
> chante le mieux.* / Mary sings well, Anne sings better than Mary,
> and Claire sings the best.

 Tip The adverb *bien* / well and the adverb *mieux* / better both contain *ie*.

Mieux is also an adjective and does not change in form.

Examples:
> *C'est mieux que jamais.* / It's better than ever.
> *Pierre est mieux avec les cheveux longs.* / Pierre looks better with
> long hair.

§5.4–7   Adjectives Used in an Adverbial Sense

An adjective used as an adverb does not normally change in form.

> *Cette rose sent bon.* / This rose smells good.
> *Ces bonbons coûtent cher.* / These candies are expensive.

§6.

Pronouns, Beginner, Intermediate, and Advanced Levels

§6.1 TYPES

§6.1–1 Subject Pronouns

The subject pronouns are:

Person	Singular	Plural
1st	*je (j')* / I	*nous* / we
2nd	*tu* / you (familiar)	*vous* / you (singular polite or plural)
3rd	{ *il* / he, it *elle* / she, it *on* / one	*ils* / they *(m.)* *elles* / they *(f.)*

- Note that *je* becomes *j'* before a vowel or a silent *h:*

  j'aime / I love; *j'hésite* / I hesitate.

- Note that the masculine plural pronoun *ils* is used when there is at least one masculine noun or male individual in a pair or group. The adjective is also masculine plural:

  Richard et Lucille sont canadiens. → *Ils* sont canadiens. / They are Canadian.

Tip

- Remember that *vous* is not always plural; it is also the polite form of the second person; *tu* is the familiar form. You can use the *tu* form with members of the family and close friends, but always use the *vous* form with strangers and with people you do not know well.You should also use the *tu* form with pets, even if you don't know them well!

§6.1–2   Direct Object Pronouns

The direct object pronouns are:

Person	Singular
1st	*me (m')* / me
2nd	*te (t')* / you (familiar)
3rd	{ *le (l')* / him, it { *la (l')* / her, it } (person or thing)

Person	Plural
1st	*nous* / us
2nd	*vous* / you (singular polite or plural)
3rd	*les* / them (persons or things)

- A direct object pronoun takes the place of a direct object noun.
- A direct object noun ordinarily comes after the verb, but a direct object pronoun is ordinarily placed *in front* of the verb or infinitive. For the position of direct and indirect object pronouns in different types of sentences, see §11.2 to §11.5.

Examples:

J'ai les lettres. / I have the letters. → *Je les ai.* / I have them.
Je connais Luigi. / I know Luigi. → *Je le connais.* / I know him.

 Tip
- *Je lis la leçon.* / I'm reading the lesson. Drop the noun *leçon;* what remains is *la*, the feminine singular definite article. It now becomes the direct object pronoun. Place it in front of the verb; *Je la lis.* / I'm reading it.

- *Me, te, le,* and *la* become *m', t', l'* when directly followed by a verb that starts with a vowel or silent *h*.

  Elle a le portable. / She has the cell phone.
  Elle l'a. / She has it.

§6.1–3 Indirect Object Pronouns

The indirect object pronouns are:

Person	Singular	
1st	*me (m')*	to me
2nd	*te (t')*	to you (familiar)
3rd	*lui*	to him, to her

Person	Plural	
1st	*nous*	to us
2nd	*vous*	to you (singular polite or plural)
3rd	*leur*	to them

- An indirect object pronoun takes the place of an indirect object noun. An indirect object noun is a noun that is used as an indirect object. Example: I am talking to Mary. In that sentence Mary is an indirect object noun because it is preceded by the preposition "to"; as an indirect object pronoun, one would say "to her" in place of "to Mary."

- An indirect object pronoun is ordinarily placed *in front* of the verb. For the position of direct and indirect object pronouns in different types of sentences, see §11.2 to §11.5.

  Examples:
  Je parle à Janine. / I'm talking to Janine. → *Je lui parle.* / I'm talking to her.
  Je parle à Luigi et à mon ami. / I'm talking to Luigi and my friend. → *Je leur parle.* / I'm talking to them.

§6.1–4 Double Object Pronouns

Tip To get a picture of what the word order is when you have more than one object pronoun (direct and indirect) in a sentence, see Order of Elements in French Sentences, §11.2 to §11.5.

§6.1–5 *En*

- The pronoun *en* takes the place of the partitive and serves as a direct object. It can refer to persons or things.

  Examples:
  Avez-vous des frères? / Do you have any brothers?
  Oui, j'en ai. / Yes, I have (some).
  Avez-vous de l'argent? / Have you any money?
  Oui, j'en ai./ Yes, I have (some). *Non, je n'en ai pas.* / No, I don't have any.

- The past participle of a compound verb does not agree with the preceding direct object *en*. See also the last paragraph in §7.1.

  Avez-vous écrit des lettres? / Did you write any letters?
  Oui, j'en ai écrit trois. / Yes, I wrote three (of them).

- When using a reflexive verb, use *en* to take the place of the preposition *de* + a thing.

Est-ce que vous vous souvenez de l'adresse? / Do you remember the address?
Oui, je m'en souviens. / Yes, I remember it.
Est-ce que vous vous servez des hors-d'œuvre? / Are you helping yourself to the hors d'œuvre?
Oui, merci, je m'en sers. / Yes, thank you, I'm helping myself to some.

Do not use *en* to take the place of the preposition *de* + a person. Use a disjunctive pronoun (see §6.1–7).

Est-ce que vous vous souvenez de cette dame? / Do you remember this lady?
Oui, je me souviens d'elle. / Yes, I remember her.

● Use *en* to take the place of *de* + noun and retain the word of quantity.

Avez-vous beaucoup d'amis? / Do you have many friends?
Oui, j'en ai beaucoup. / Yes, I have many (of them).
Madame Paquet a-t-elle mis trop de sel dans le ragoût? / Did Mrs. Paquet put too much salt in the stew?
Oui, elle en a mis trop dans le ragoût. / Yes, she put too much (of it) in the stew.

● Use *en* to take the place of the preposition *de* + the place to mean "from there."

Est-ce que vous venez de l'école? / Are you coming from school?
Oui, j'en viens. / Yes, I'm coming from there.
Non, je n'en viens pas. / No, I am not coming from there.

§6.1–6   *Y*

Use *y* as a pronoun to serve as an object replacing a prepositional phrase beginning with *à, dans, sur,* or *chez* that refers to things, places, or ideas.

Est-ce que vous pensez à l'examen? / Are you thinking of the exam?
Oui, j'y pense. / Yes, I'm thinking of it.
Je réponds à la lettre. / I'm answering the letter.
J'y réponds. / I'm answering it.

Est-ce que les fleurs sont sur la table? / Are the flowers on the
   table?
Oui, elles y sont. / Yes, they are there.
Est-ce que vous allez chez Pierre? / Are you going to Pierre's?
Oui, j'y vais. / Yes, I'm going (there).

§6.1–7 Disjunctive Pronouns

Person	Singular	Plural
1st	*moi* me, I	*nous* us, we
2nd	*toi* you (familiar)	*vous* you (formal singular or plural)
3rd	{ *soi* oneself { *lui* him, he { *elle* her, she	{ *eux* them, they (m.) { *elles* them, they (f.)

| Tip | *Je vais chez moi.* / I'm going to my house.
Tu vas chez toi. / You're going to your house.
Il va chez lui. / He's going to his house.
Elle va chez elle. / She's going to her house.
On va chez soi. / One is going to one's own house.
Nous allons chez nous. / We're going to our house.
Vous allez chez vous. / You're going to your house.
Ils vont chez eux. / They're going to their house.
Elles vont chez elles. / They're going to their house.

A disjunctive pronoun is used:

• as object of a preposition.

   Elle parle avec moi. / She is talking with me.
   Je pense toujours à toi. / I always think of you.

• in a compound subject or object.

   Elle et lui sont amoureux. / He and she are in love.
   Je vous connais—toi et lui. / I know you—you and him.

- for emphasis.

  Moi, je parle bien; lui, il ne parle pas bien. / I speak well; he does not speak well.

- to indicate possession with *à* if the verb is *être* and if the subject is a noun, personal pronoun, or demonstrative pronoun.

  Ce livre est à moi. / This book is mine.
  Je suis à toi. / I am yours.

- with *c'est* and *ce sont*.

  Qui est à la porte?—C'est moi. / Who is at the door? It is I.
  C'est toi? Oui, c'est moi. / Is it you? Yes, it is I.
  Est-ce que ce sont eux?—Oui, ce sont eux. / Is it they?—Yes it's they.

 Tip In spoken English we often say, "It's me. It's her. It's him," and so on instead of "It is I. It is she. It is he." In French, one must always say, "*C'est moi. C'est elle. C'est lui,*" and so on.

- with *même* and *mêmes*.

  Est-ce Pierre?—Oui, c'est lui-même. / Is it Peter? Yes, it's he himself.
  Vont-ils les manger eux-mêmes? / Are they going to eat them themselves?

- when no verb is stated.

  Qui est à l'appareil? Moi. / Who is on the phone? I (am).
  Qui a brisé le vase? Eux. / Who broke the vase? They (did).

See also Order of Elements in French Sentences, §11.

§6.1–8 Demonstrative Pronouns

The demonstrative pronouns are:

	Singular	**Plural**
Masculine	*celui* / the one	*ceux* / the ones
Feminine	*celle* / the one	*celles* / the ones

Examples:

J'ai mangé mon gâteau et celui de Pierre. / I ate my cake and Peter's.

Il aime beaucoup ma voiture et celle de Jacques. / He likes my car very much and Jack's.

J'ai mangé mes petits pois et ceux de David. / I ate my peas and David's.

J'aime tes jupes et celles de Jeanne. / I like your skirts and Joan's.

J'ai deux éclairs; est-ce que tu préfères celui-ci ou celui-là? / I have two eclairs; do you prefer this one or that one?

J'ai deux pommes; est-ce que tu préfères celle-ci ou celle-là? / I have two apples; do you prefer this one or that one?

Tip

Quel chapeau? Celui que tu as acheté. / Which hat? The one (that) you bought.

Note that in English we do not have to say *that*, but in French we must say *que* because a new clause follows.

Tip

Quelles fleurs? Celles que tu m'as données. / Which flowers? The ones (that) you gave me.

Tip

BUT:

Qui l'a fait? C'est lui qui l'a fait. / Who did it? He's the one who did it.

Tip

C'est elle qui l'a dit. / She's the one who said it.

ce (c'), *ceci, cela, ça*

These are demonstrative pronouns but they are invariable; that is, they do not change in gender and number. They refer to things that are not identified by name and may refer to an idea or a statement mentioned.

Examples:

C'est vrai. / It's true.

*Ceci est vrai. / This is true. *Ceci est faux.* / This is false.

*Cela est vrai. / That is true. *Cela est faux.* / That is false.

Ça m'intéresse beaucoup. / That interests me very much.

Qu'est-ce que c'est que cela? OR *Qu'est-ce que c'est que ça?* /
What's that?

Note that *cela* shortens to *ça* when used informally.

* Note also that *ceci* refers to what follows and *cela* to what
was stated.

§6.1–9 Indefinite Pronouns

aucun (aucune) / not any, not one, none

un autre (une autre) / another, another one

nous autres Français / we French (people)

nous autres Américains / we American (people)

certains (certaines) / certain ones

chacun (chacune) / each one

nul (nulle) / not one, not any, none

n'importe qui, n'importe quel / anyone

n'importe quoi / anything

on / people, one, they, you, we

> *On dit qu'il va pleuvoir.* / They say (that) it's going to rain.

personne / no one, nobody

plusieurs / several

> *J'en ai plusieurs.* / I have several (of them).

quelque chose / something

quelqu'un (quelqu'une) / someone, somebody

quelques-uns (quelques-unes) / some, a few

quiconque / whoever, whosoever

soi / oneself

> *On est chez soi dans cet hôtel.* / People feel at home in this hotel.

tout / all, everything

> *Tout est bien qui finit bien.* / All is well that ends well.

§6.1–10   Interrogative Pronouns

Referring to Persons

- As subject of a verb:

    Qui est à l'appareil? / Who is on the phone?
    Qui est-ce qui est à l'appareil? / Who is on the phone?
    Lequel des deux garçons arrive? / Which (one) of the two boys is
      arriving?
    Laquelle des deux jeunes filles est ici? / Which (one) of the two
      girls is here?

- As direct object of a verb:

    Qui aimez-vous? / Whom do you love?
    Qui est-ce que vous aimez? / Whom do you love?
    Lequel de ces deux garçons aimez-vous? / Which (one) of these
      two boys do you love?
    Laquelle de ces deux jeunes filles aimez-vous? / Which (one) of
      these two girls do you love?

- As object of a preposition:

    Avec qui allez-vous au cinéma? / With whom are you going to the
      movies?
    A qui parlez-vous au téléphone? / To whom are you talking on the
      telephone?

Note that when the interrogative pronouns *lequel (laquelle),
lesquels (lesquelles)* are objects of the prepositions *à* or *de*,
their forms are:

Singular	Plural
auquel (à laquelle)	*auxquels (auxquelles)*
duquel (de laquelle)	*desquels (desquelles)*

    Auquel de ces deux garçons parlez-vous? / To which (one) of
      these two boys are you talking?
    A laquelle de ces deux jeunes filles parlez-vous? / To which (one)
      of these two girls are you talking?

Auxquels de ces hommes parlez-vous? / To which (ones) of these
  men do you talk?
Auxquelles de ces femmes parlez-vous? / To which (ones) of
  these women are you talking?
Duquel de ces deux garçons parlez-vous? / About which (one) of
  these two boys are you talking?

Referring to Things

• As subject of a verb:

Qu'est-ce qui est arrivé? / What arrived? OR What happened?
Qu'est-ce qui s'est passé? / What happened?

> **Tip** — *Une devinette avec qu'est-ce qui*
>
> *Qu'est-ce qui vous appartient et dont les autres se servent
> souvent?* / What belongs to you that others use often?
> *votre nom* / your name

Laquelle de ces deux voitures marche bien? / Which (one) of
  these two cars runs well?
Lesquels de tous ces trains sont modernes? / Which (ones) of all
  these trains are modern?

• As direct object of a verb:

Que faites-vous? / What are you doing?
Qu'a-t-elle? / What does she have? OR What's the matter with
  her?
Qu'est-ce que vous faites? / What are you doing?
Laquelle de ces voitures préférez-vous? / Which (one) of these
  cars do you prefer?

• As object of a preposition:

Avec quoi écrivez-vous? / With what are you writing?
A quoi pensez-vous? / Of what are you thinking? OR What are you
  thinking of?

§6.1–11   Possessive Pronouns

MASCULINE			
Singular		**Plural**	
le mien	mine	*les miens*	mine
le tien	yours (familiar)	*les tiens*	yours (familiar)
le sien	his, hers, its	*les siens*	his, hers, its
le nôtre	ours	*les nôtres*	ours
le vôtre	yours	*les vôtres*	yours
le leur	theirs	*les leurs*	theirs

FEMININE			
Singular		**Plural**	
la mienne	mine	*les miennes*	mine
la tienne	yours (familiar)	*les tiennes*	yours (familiar)
la sienne	his, hers, its	*les siennes*	his, hers, its
la nôtre	ours	*les nôtres*	ours
la vôtre	yours	*les vôtres*	yours
la leur	theirs	*les leurs*	theirs

- A possessive pronoun takes the place of a possessive adjective + noun.

   mon livre / my book; *le mien* / mine.

- A possessive pronoun agrees in gender and number with what it is replacing.

   son livre / his (her) book; *le sien* / his (hers).

- When the definite articles *le* and *les* are preceded by the prepositions *à* and *de*, they combine as follows: *au mien, aux miens, du mien, des miens.*

Paul me parle de ses parents et je lui parle des miens. / Paul is
  talking to me about his parents and I am talking to him about
  mine.

Je préfère ma voiture à la tienne. / I prefer my car to yours.

- Possessive pronouns are used with *être* to emphasize a
  distinction.

  Ce livre-ci est le mien et celui-là est le tien. / This book is mine
    and that one is yours.

- If no distinction is made as to who owns what, use *être* + *à*
  + disjunctive pronoun. (§6.1–7)

  Ce livre est à lui. / This book is his.

- Instead of using the possessive pronouns in French, we say
  "one of my friends," "one of my books," etc.

  un de mes amis / a friend of mine; *un de mes livres* / a book of
    mine
  une de ses amies / a girlfriend of his (hers)
  un de nos amis / a friend of ours

§6.1–12   Reflexive Pronouns

- The reflexive pronouns, which are used with reflexive verbs,
  are *me, te, se, nous,* and *vous.*
- The corresponding English pronouns are: myself, yourself,
  herself, himself, oneself, itself, ourselves, yourselves,
  themselves.
- To form the present tense of a reflexive verb in a simple
  affirmative sentence, put the reflexive pronoun in front of the
  verb.

  Je me lave. / I wash myself.

- A reflexive verb expresses an action that turns back upon
  the subject.

  Jacqueline se lave tous les jours. / Jacqueline washes herself
    every day.

You must be careful to use the appropriate reflexive pronoun—the one that matches the subject pronoun. You already know the subject pronouns, but here they are again, beside the reflexive pronouns.

Person	Singular	Plural
1st	*je me lave*	*nous nous lavons*
2nd	*tu te laves*	*vous vous lavez*
3rd	*il se lave* *elle se lave* *on se lave*	*ils se lavent* *elles se lavent*

 To get a picture of what the word order is when you have more than one pronoun of any kind in a sentence, see Order of Elements in French Sentences (§11.).

§6.1–13 Relative Pronouns

 A *relative pronoun* is a word that refers to an antecedent. An *antecedent* is something that comes before something; it can be a word, a phrase, a clause that is replaced by a pronoun or some other substitute. For example, in the sentence "Is it Mary who did that?" "who" is the relative pronoun and "Mary" is the antecedent. Another example: "It seems to me that you are wrong, which is what I had suspected right along." The relative pronoun is "which" and the antecedent is the clause, "that you are wrong."

Some common relative pronouns are:

- *dont* / of whom, of which, whose, whom, which

  Voici le livre dont j'ai besoin. / Here is the book (that) I need.
  Monsieur Béry, dont le fils est avocat, est maintenant en France. /
    Mr. Béry, whose son is a lawyer, is now in France.

- *ce dont* / what, of which, that of which

  Je ne trouve pas ce dont j'ai besoin. / I don't find what I need.
  Ce dont vous parlez est absurde. / What you are talking about is
    absurd.

- *ce que (ce qu')* / what, that which

  Comprenez-vous ce que je vous dis? / Do you understand what I
    am telling you?
  Comprenez-vous ce qu'elle vous dit? / Do you understand what
    she is saying to you?
  Je comprends ce que vous dîtes et je comprends ce qu'elle dit. /
    I understand what you are saying and I understand what she is
    saying.

- *ce qui* / what, that which

  Ce qui est vrai est vrai. / What is true is true.
  Je ne sais pas ce qui s'est passé. / I don't know what happened.

Note that *ce qui* is a subject.

- *lequel* (in all its forms) / which

  As a relative pronoun, *lequel* (in its various forms) is used
as object of a preposition referring to things.

  *Donnez-moi un autre morceau de papier sur lequel je puisse
    écrire mon adresse.* / Give me another piece of paper on which
    I can write my address.

- *où* / where, in which, on which, when

  Aimez-vous la salle à manger où nous mangeons? / Do you like
    the dining room where we eat?
  Je vais ouvrir le tiroir où j'ai mis l'argent. / I am going to open the
    drawer where I put the money.
  Il faisait beau le jour où elle est née. / The weather was nice the
    day (when) she was born.

• *que* or *qu'* / whom, which, that

> *Le garçon que vous voyez là-bas est mon meilleur ami.* / The boy
> (whom) you see over there is my best friend.
> *La composition qu'elle a écrite est excellente.* / The composition
> (that) she wrote is excellent.

Tip

Note that the relative pronoun *que* (whom, which, or
that) must be used in French but in English it is not
always stated.

• *qui* / who, whom, which, that

> *Connais-tu la jeune fille qui parle avec mon frère?* / Do you know
> the girl who is talking with my brother?
> *Avez-vous une bicyclette qui marche bien?* / Do you have a
> bicycle that (which) runs well?

§6.1–14 *C'est* + adjective + *à* + infinitive

> *C'est difficile à faire.* / It is difficult to do.

Use this construction when what is being referred to *has
already been mentioned*.

Examples:

> *Le devoir pour demain est difficile, n'est-ce pas?* / The homework
> for tomorrow is difficult, isn't it?
> *Oui, c'est difficile à faire.* / Yes, it [the homework] is difficult to do.
>
> *J'aimerais créer un site Web.* / I would like to create a Web site.
> *C'est facile à faire! Je vais vous montrer.* / It's easy to do! I'll show you.

§6.1–15 *Il est* + adjective + *de* + infinitive

> *Il est impossible de lire ce gros livre en une heure.* / It is impossi-
> ble to read this thick book within one hour.

Use this construction when the thing that is impossible, or
difficult, or easy (or any adjective) to do is mentioned in the
same sentence at the same time.

§6.1–16 Neuter Pronoun *le*

The word *le* is the masculine singular definite article. It is also
the masculine singular direct object. *Le* is used as a neuter
pronoun and functions as a direct object referring to an
adjective, a phrase, a clause, or a complete statement. It is
generally not translated into English, except to mean "it" or
"so."

> *Janine est jolie, mais Henriette ne l'est pas.* / Janine is pretty, but
>   Henrietta isn't.
> *Moi, je crois qu'ils vont gagner le match, et vous? Je le crois
>   aussi.* / I think they are going to win the game, and you? I think
>   so too.

Tip

To get a picture of what the word order is when you
have more than one pronoun of any kind in a
sentence, see Order of Elements in French
Sentences, §11.2 to §11.5.

Tip

Une devinette / a riddle

*J'ai un chapeau, mais je n'ai pas de tête. Ne
trouvez-vous pas que c'est bête?* / I have a hat, but
I don't have a head.
   Don't you think it's stupid?

un champignon / a mushroom

§7.
Verbs, Beginner, Intermediate, and Advanced Levels

For a summary of the names of verb tenses and moods in French with English equivalents, see page 129.

§7.1 AGREEMENT

SUBJECT AND VERB

A subject and its corresponding verb form must agree in *person* (first, second, or third) and number (singular or plural).

Example:
Je vais au cinéma. / I'm going to the movies.

SUBJECT AND REFLEXIVE PRONOUN OF A REFLEXIVE VERB

A subject and reflexive pronoun must agree in person and number.

Example:
Je me lave tous les matins. / I wash myself every morning.

SUBJECT AND PAST PARTICIPLE OF AN *ÊTRE* VERB

The past participle of an *être* verb agrees with the subject in gender and number.

Elle est allée au cinéma. / She went to the movies. OR She has gone to the movies.
Elles sont allées au cinéma. / They went to the movies. OR They have gone to the movies.

49

PRECEDING REFLEXIVE PRONOUN AND PAST PARTICIPLE OF A REFLEXIVE VERB

> *Elle s'est lavée.* / She washed herself.
> *Elles se sont lavées.* / They washed themselves.

However, there is *no* agreement made with the past participle of a reflexive verb if the reflexive pronoun serves as an indirect object pronoun. In the following example, *se (s')* is the indirect object; *les mains* is the direct object.

> *Elle s'est lavé les mains.* / She washed her hands.
> *Elles se sont lavé les mains.* / They washed their hands.

Note this:

> *Elles se sont regardées.* / They looked at each other.

Here, the reflexive pronoun *se* serves as the direct object. How do you know? There is no other obvious direct object mentioned, so what they looked at was *se* (each other); of course, you have to look at the subject to see what the gender and number is of the reflexive pronoun *se* in the sentence you are dealing with. The action of the verb is reciprocal.

Remember that the verb *regarder* in French means "to look at" in English; the preposition "at" is not expressed with *à* in French; it is included in the verb—that is why we are dealing with the reflexive pronoun as a direct object here, not an indirect object pronoun.

This same sentence, *Elles se sont regardées*, might also mean: "They looked at themselves." The principle of agreement is still the same. If you mean to say "They looked at each other," in order to avoid two meanings, add *l'une et l'autre*. If more than two persons, add *les unes les autres*.

And note:

> *Elles se sont parlé au téléphone.* / They talked to each other on the telephone.

Here, the reflexive pronoun *se* is the indirect object because they spoke to each other; *parler à* is what you are dealing with here.

No agreement is made on a past participle with an indirect object. You must remember that.

PAST PARTICIPLE OF AN *AVOIR* VERB WITH A PRECEDING DIRECT OBJECT

Examples:

> *Je l'ai vue au concert.* / I saw her at the concert.

- There is agreement on the past participle (*vue*) because the preceding direct object is *la (l')*. Agreement is made in gender and number.

> *Aimez-vous les fleurs que je vous ai données?* / Do you like the flowers (that) I gave you?

- There is agreement on the past participle *(données)* of this *avoir* verb because there is a preceding direct object, *les fleurs*; the relative pronoun *que* refers to *les fleurs*. Since this direct object noun precedes the verb, the past participle must agree in gender and number. A preceding direct object, therefore, can be a pronoun or noun.

> *Quels films avez-vous vus?* / What films did you see?

- There is agreement on the past participle *(vus)* of this *avoir* verb because the preceding direct object, *films*, is a masculine plural noun.

> *Avez-vous mangé les pâtisseries?* / Did you eat the pastries?
> *Oui, je les ai mangées.* / Yes, I ate them.

- In the response to this question, there is agreement on the past participle *(mangées)* of this *avoir* verb because the preceding direct object, *les*, refers to *les pâtisseries*, a feminine plural noun.

> *J'en ai mangé assez.* / I ate enough (of them).

- There is no agreement on the past participle *(mangé)* of this *avoir* verb because the preceding direct object is, in this sentence, the pronoun *en*. We do not normally make an agreement with *en*, whether it precedes or follows. This is an exception. Review §6.1–5 *En*.

§7.2 PAST PARTICIPLE

REGULAR FORMATION

Infinitive	Type Ending	Drop	Add	Past Participle
donner	*-er*	*-er*	*é*	*donné*
finir	*-ir*	*-ir*	*i*	*fini*
vendre	*-re*	*-re*	*u*	*vendu*

COMMON IRREGULAR PAST PARTICIPLES

Infinitive	Past Participle
apprendre	*appris*
asseoir	*assis*
avoir	*eu*
boire	*bu*

Infinitive	Past Participle
comprendre	compris
conduire	conduit
connaître	connu
construire	construit
courir	couru
couvrir	couvert
craindre	craint
croire	cru
devenir	devenu
devoir	dû
dire	dit
écrire	écrit
être	été
faire	fait
falloir	fallu
lire	lu
mettre	mis
mourir	mort
naître	né
offrir	offert
ouvrir	ouvert
paraître	paru
permettre	permis
plaire	plu
pleuvoir	plu
pouvoir	pu
prendre	pris
promettre	promis
recevoir	reçu
revenir	revenu
rire	ri
savoir	su

Infinitive	Past Participle
suivre	*suivi*
taire	*tu*
tenir	*tenu*
valoir	*valu*
venir	*venu*
vivre	*vécu*
voir	*vu*
vouloir	*voulu*

§7.3 TYPES

§7.3–1 Helping Verbs (Auxiliary Verbs) *avoir* and *être*

Most verbs use **avoir** as the helping verb in the **passé composé**. However, a number of verbs, in addition to reflexive verbs, use **être** as the helping verb. The most common ones are:

aller (to go)
arriver (to arrive)
descendre (to go down, come down)
devenir (to become)
entrer (to enter)
monter (to go up, come up)
mourir (to die)
naître (to be born)
partir (to leave)
passer (to go by, pass by)
rentrer (to go in again, to return home)

rester (to remain, stay)
retourner (to return, go back)
revenir (to come back)
sortir (to go out)
tomber (to fall)
venir (to come)

Tip	Most French verbs are conjugated with *avoir* to form a compound tense. All reflexive verbs, such as *se laver,* are conjugated with *être.*

Tip	If you're having some trouble choosing your helping verb in the **passé composé**, just remember APEMAN, which is a tip to help you remember the French verbs we are dealing with in this unit. Most of the verbs in this list are intransitive and use **être** as a helping verb. As you will see below, a few of them sometimes take a direct object, in which case you should use **avoir**.

Here is a way to break down the verbs that use **être** as a helping verb into smaller groups. Note the general similarity in the type of action described by the verbs in each APEMAN group.

Aller/Venir-Devenir-Revenir
Passer/Rester
Entrer-Rentrer/Sortir
Monter/Descendre/Tomber
Arriver/Partir/Retourner
Naître/Mourir

Look at the above acrostic formed by the first letter of each group. That's right: it's APEMAN! It is helpful to discuss the connections between the verbs in each of these groups.

> Early modern humans created the cave paintings in the *grotte de Lascaux* (the Lascaux Cave) in Dordogne, in southwest France, over 17,000 years ago.

You may come up with a way that works better for you. This way of looking at the "**être** verbs" is not set in stone—or the Stone Age. It's a tool to help you organize your study. The best way to remember which verbs use **être** as a helping verb in the **passé composé** is to practice using them!

A
Aller/Venir-Devenir-Revenir
Aller and **venir** are used to talk about opposite movements:
Marie est allée au supermarché.
Marie went to the supermarket.
Les Gosselin sont venus chez nous hier soir.
The Gosselins came to our home yesterday evening.

The verbs based on **venir** follow the same pattern in the **passé composé**:
Ma mère est devenue pédiatre pour aider les enfants.
My mother became a pediatrician to help children.
Est-ce que Pierre est revenu de l'école?
Has Peter come back from school?

However, **prévenir** (to warn) uses **avoir** in the **passé composé**:
J'ai prévenu ma soeur qu'on annonçait de la pluie.
I warned my sister that they were predicting rain.

P

Passer uses **être** as its auxiliary when it has no direct object (see §7.3–3):

Jean-Claude est passé au bureau de sa directrice.

Jean-Claude went by his director's office.

But **passer** uses **avoir** when it is used transitively (that is, with a direct object):

Elle m'a passé le sel. (direct object = le sel)

She passed me the salt. / She passed the salt to me.

Rester takes **être** as its auxiliary in the **passé composé**.

While **passer** means to pass by, **rester** means "to stay." Well, they're not quite opposites:

Sabrina est restée à la maison parce qu'elle était malade.

Sabrina stayed at home because she was sick.

E

Entrer-Rentrer/Sortir

Entrer and **sortir** are antonyms. **Être** is the helping verb when you use **entrer** in the **passé composé**:

Nous sommes entrés par la porte principale.

We came in by the main door.

When it has no direct object, **rentrer** (to go in again, to return home) also uses **être** as its helping verb in the **passé composé**:

Anne et Marie sont rentrées à 23h.

Anne and Mary returned at 11 P.M.

But when **rentrer** takes a direct object, you must use **avoir** as the helping verb:

Frédéric a rentré le chat avant de fermer la porte.

Fred brought the cat inside before closing the door.

Sortir is the antonym of **entrer**, and it also uses **être** as its helping verb in the **passé composé**.

Jeanne est sortie avec ses amis.

Jean went out with her friends.

However, if **sortir** takes a direct object, you must use **avoir** as the helping verb:

David a sorti son portefeuille pour chercher sa carte de crédit.
David took out his wallet to look for his credit card.

M
Monter/Descendre/Tomber

These three verbs are used to describe up or down movement. When **monter** and **descendre** are used intransitively (without a direct object), they use **être** as the helping verb:

Elle est montée lentement.
She went up slowly.
Elle est descendue vite.
She came down quickly.

When they are used transitively (with a direct object), these verbs take **avoir** as the helping verb:

Elle a monté l'escalier.
She went up the stairs.
Elle a descendu la valise.
She brought down the suitcase.

Tomber is almost always used intransitively and therefore usually takes **être** as its helping verb in the **passé composé**:
Elle est tombée dans l'escalier.
She fell in the staircase.

A
Arriver/Partir/Retourner

This group of verbs is used for arrivals and departures. They take the helping verb **être** in the **passé composé.**

Madeleine est arrivée.
Madeleine arrived.
Francine est partie.
Francine left.

Mes parents sont retournés.
My parents returned.

However, when **retourner** takes a direct object (meaning to turn over, to turn around), you should use **avoir** as the helping verb:

Quand Jean a retourné la pierre, il a trouvé ses clés.
When John turned over the stone, he found his keys.

N
Naître/Mourir

Finally, we have **naître** and its antonym, **mourir**. Both verbs take the helping verb **être** in the **passé composé**:

Ma tante est née en 1965.
My aunt was born in 1965.
Charles de Gaulle est mort en 1970.
Charles de Gaulle died in 1970.

§7.3–2 Transitive Verbs

A transitive verb is a verb that can take a direct object. It is transitive because the action passes over and directly affects something or someone in some way.

Je vois mon ami. / I see my friend. → *Je le vois.* / I see him.
Je ferme la fenêtre. / I am closing the window. → *Je la ferme.* / I'm closing it.

When the direct object of the verb is a pronoun, it is usually placed in front of the verb. The only time it is placed after the verb is in the affirmative imperative. To get an idea of the position of direct object pronouns see Order of Elements in French Sentences, §11.2 to §11.5.

§7.3–3   Intransitive Verbs

An intransitive verb is a verb that does not take a direct object. Such a verb is called intransitive because the action does not pass over and directly affect anyone or anything.

> *La maîtresse parle.* / The teacher is talking.
> *Elle est partie tôt.* / She left early.
> *Elles sont descendues vite.* / They came down quickly.
> *Nous sommes montées lentement.* / We went up slowly.

An intransitive verb can take an indirect object.

> *La maîtresse parle aux élèves.* / The teacher is talking to the students.

Here the indirect object noun is *élèves* because it is preceded by *aux* / to the.

> *La maîtresse leur parle.* / The teacher is talking to them.

Here the indirect object is the pronoun *leur*, meaning "to them."

§7.4   PRESENT PARTICIPLE

Regular Formation

The present participle is regularly formed in the following way: Take the *nous* form of the present indicative tense of the verb you have in mind, drop the first person plural ending *-ons*, and add *-ant*. That ending is equivalent to *-ing* in English.

Infinitive	Present Tense 1st Person Pl.	Drop -ons	Add -ant	Present Participle
finir / to finish	*nous finissons*	finiss	ant	finissant
manger / to eat	*nous mangeons*	mange	ant	mangeant
vendre / to sell	*nous vendons*	vend	ant	vendant
faire / to do; make	*nous faisons*	fais	ant	faisant
dire / to say; tell	*nous disons*	dis	ant	disant

Common Irregular Present Participles

Infinitive	Present Participle
avoir to have	ayant
être to be	étant
savoir to know	sachant

Tip	If you're not sure which is a present participle and which is a past participle in French, associate the n in present with the *n* in the French ending *-ant* of a present participle.

En + Present Participle

The present participle in French is used primarily with the preposition *en*, meaning "on," "upon," "in," "while," "by."

> *en chantant* / while singing
> *en finissant* / upon finishing
> *en vendant* / by selling
> *en mangeant* / upon eating, while eating
> *en voyageant* / by traveling
> *en ayant* / on having
> *en étant* / on being, upon being
> *en sachant* / upon knowing

The present participle is sometimes used as an adjective.

> *un enfant amusant* / an amusing child (boy)
> *une enfant amusante* / an amusing child (girl)

§7.5 VERBS AND PREPOSITIONS

In this section you will learn what preposition goes with what verb.

Verb + *à* + Noun or Pronoun

- *assister à quelque chose (à une assemblée, à une réunion, à un spectacle, etc.)* / to attend or be present at (a gathering, a meeting, a theatrical presentation, etc.)

  Allez-vous assister à la conférence du professeur Godard? / Are you going to attend (be present at) Professor Godard's lecture?—*Oui, je vais y assister.* / Yes, I am going to attend it.

- *demander à quelqu'un* / to ask someone

  Demandez à la dame où s'arrête l'autobus. / Ask the lady where the bus stops.

- *désobéir à quelqu'un* / to disobey someone

  Ce chien ne désobéit jamais à son maître. / This dog never disobeys his master.
  Il ne lui désobéit jamais. / He never disobeys him.

- *être à quelqu'un* / to belong to someone

  Ce livre est à Victor. / This book belongs to Victor.

- *faire attention à quelqu'un ou à quelque chose* / to pay attention to someone or to something

  Faites attention au professeur. / Pay attention to the professor.

- *s'intéresser à quelqu'un ou à quelque chose* / to be interested in someone or something

  Je m'intéresse aux sports. / I am interested in sports.

- *jouer à* / to play (a game or sport)

  Il aime bien jouer à la balle. / He likes to play ball.
  Elle aime bien jouer au tennis. / She likes to play tennis.

- *obéir à quelqu'un* / to obey someone

  Une personne honorable obéit à ses parents. / An honorable person obeys his (her) parents.

- *participer à quelque chose* / to participate in something

  Je participe aux sports. / I participate in sports.

- *penser à quelqu'un ou à quelque chose* / to think of (about) someone or something

  Je pense à mes amis. / I am thinking of my friends.
  Je pense à eux. / I am thinking of them.
  Je pense à mon travail. / I am thinking about my work.
  J'y pense. / I am thinking about it.

- *répondre à quelqu'un ou à quelque chose* / to answer someone or something

  J'ai répondu au professeur. / I answered the teacher.
  Je lui ai répondu. / I answered him.
  J'ai répondu à la lettre. / I answered the letter.
  J'y al répondu. / I answered It.

- *ressembler à quelqu'un* / to resemble someone

  Il ressemble beaucoup à sa mère. / He resembles his mother a lot.

- *réussir à quelque chose* / to succeed in something
  réussir à un examen / to pass an examination

  Il a réussi à l'examen. / He passed the exam.

- *téléphoner à quelqu'un* / to telephone someone

  Marie a téléphoné à Paul. / Marie telephoned Paul.
  Elle lui a téléphoné. / She telephoned him.

Verb + *à* + Infinitive

- *aider à* / to help

    Roger aide son petit frère à faire son devoir de mathématiques.
    Roger is helping his little brother to do his math homework.

- *s'amuser à* / to amuse oneself, enjoy, have fun

    Il y a des élèves qui s'amusent à mettre le professeur en colère. /
    There are pupils who enjoy making the teacher angry.

- *apprendre à* / to learn

    J'apprends à lire. / I am learning to read.

- *s'attendre à* / to expect

    Je m'attendais à trouver une salle de classe vide. / I was
    expecting to find an empty classroom.

- *avoir à* / to have to, to be obliged to (do something)

    J'ai mes devoirs à faire ce soir. / I have to do my homework
    tonight.

- *commencer à* / to begin

    Il commence à pleuvoir. / It is beginning to rain.

- *continuer à* / to continue

    Je continue à étudier le français. / I am continuing to study
    French.

- *décider quelqu'un à* / to persuade someone

    J'ai décidé mon père à me prêter quelques euros. / I persuaded
    my father to lend me a few euros.

- *se décider à* / to make up one's mind

    Il s'est décidé à l'épouser. / He made up his mind to marry her.

- *demander à* / to ask, request

    Elle demande à parler. / She asks to speak.

- *encourager à* / to encourage

    Je l'ai encouragé à suivre un cours de français. / I encouraged
    him to take a course in French.

- *enseigner à* / to teach

    Je vous enseigne à lire en français. / I am teaching you to read in
    French.

- *s'habituer à* / to get used (to)

    Je m'habitue à parler français couramment. / I am getting used to speaking French fluently.

- *hésiter à* / to hesitate

    J'hésite à répondre à sa lettre. / I hesitate to reply to her (his) letter.

- *inviter à* / to invite

    Monsieur et Madame Boivin ont invité les Béry à dîner chez eux. / Mr. and Mrs. Boivin invited the Bérys to have dinner at their house.

- *se mettre à* / to begin

    L'enfant se met à rire. / The child is beginning to laugh.

- *parvenir à* / to succeed

    Elle est parvenue à être docteur. / She succeeded in becoming a doctor.

- *se plaire à* / to take pleasure in

    Il se plaît à taquiner ses amis. / He takes pleasure in teasing his friends.

- *recommencer à* / to begin again

    Il recommence à pleuvoir. / It is beginning to rain again.

- *réussir à* / to succeed in

    Henri a réussi à me convaincre. / Henry succeeded in convincing me.

- *songer à* / to dream; to think

    Elle songe à diriger une entreprise. / She is dreaming of running a business.

- *tenir à* / to insist, be anxious

    Je tiens absolument à voir mon enfant immédiatement. / I am very anxious to see my child immediately.

Verb + *de* + Noun

- *s'agir de* / to be a question of, a matter of

    Il s'agit de l'amour. / It is a matter of love.

- *s'approcher de* / to approach

    La dame s'approche de la porte et elle l'ouvre. / The lady
      approaches the door and opens it.

- *changer de* / to change

    Je dois changer de train à Paris. / I have to change trains in Paris.

- *se douter de* / to suspect

    Je me doute de ses opinions. / I suspect his (her) opinions.

- *féliciter de* / to congratulate on

    Je vous félicite de vos progrès. / I congratulate you on your
      progress.

- *jouer de* / to play (a musical instrument)

    Je sais jouer du piano. / I know how to play the piano.

- *manquer de* / to lack

    Cette personne manque de politesse. / This person lacks
      courtesy.

- *se méfier de* / to distrust, to mistrust, to beware of

    Je me méfie des personnes que je ne connais pas. / I distrust
      persons whom I do not know.

- *se moquer de* / to make fun of

    Les enfants aiment se moquer d'un singe. / Children like to make
      fun of a monkey.

- *s'occuper de* / to be busy with

    Madame Boulanger s'occupe de son mari infirme. / Mrs.
      Boulanger is busy with her disabled husband.
    Je m'occupe de mes affaires. / I mind my own business.
    Occupez-vous de vos affaires! / Mind your own business!

- *partir de* / to leave

    Il est parti de la maison à huit heures. / He left the house at eight
      o'clock.

- *se plaindre de* / to complain about

    Il se plaint toujours de son travail. / He always complains about
      his work.

* *remercier de* / to thank

    Je vous remercie de votre bonté. / I thank you for your kindness.

| Tip | (Use *remercier de* + an abstract noun or infinitive; *remercier pour* + a concrete object; e.g., *Je vous remercie pour le cadeau.* / I thank you for the present.) |

---

* *se rendre compte de* / to realize, to be aware of

    Je me rends compte de la condition de cette personne. / I am aware of the condition of this person.

* *se servir de* / to employ, use, make use of

    Je me sers d'un stylo quand j'écris une lettre. / I use a pen when I write a letter.

* *se souvenir de* / to remember

    Oui, je me souviens de Gervaise. / Yes, I remember Gervaise.
    Je me souviens de lui. / I remember him.
    Je me souviens d'elle. / I remember her.
    Je me souviens de l'été passé. / I remember last summer.
    Je m'en souviens. / I remember it.

* *tenir de* / to take after (to resemble)

    Julie tient de sa mère. / Julie takes after her mother.

Verb + *de* + Infinitive

* *s'agir de* / to be a question of, a matter of (This verb is impersonal.)

    Il s'agit de faire les devoirs tous les jours. / It is a matter of doing the homework every day.

* *avoir peur de* / to be afraid of

    Le petit garçon a peur de traverser la rue seul. / The little boy is afraid of crossing the street alone.

* *cesser de* / to stop, cease

    Il a cessé de pleuvoir. / It has stopped raining.

- *craindre de* / to be afraid of, fear

    La petite fille craint de traverser la rue seule. / The little girl is afraid of crossing the street alone.

- *décider de* / to decide

    J'ai décidé de partir tout de suite. / I decided to leave immediately.

- *demander de* / to ask, request

    Je vous demande de parler. / I am asking you to speak.

Tip	[Note that here the subjects are different: *I* am asking *you* to speak; but when the subjects are the same, use *demander à: Elle demande à parler.* / She is asking to speak.]

- *se dépêcher de* / to hurry

    Je me suis dépêché de venir chez vous pour vous dire quelque chose. / I hurried to come to your place in order to tell you something.

- *empêcher de* / to keep from, prevent

    Je vous empêche de sortir. / I prevent you from going out.

- essayer de / to try (When you conjugate a verb that ends in **-ayer**, you may change **y** to **i** in front of a mute **e**. You may also keep the **y**.)

    J'essaie d'ouvrir la porte mais je ne peux pas. / I'm trying to open the door but I can't.

- *féliciter de* / to congratulate

    On m'a félicité d'avoir gagné le prix. / I was congratulated on having won the prize.

- *finir de* / to finish

    J'ai fini de travailler sur cette composition. / I have finished working on this composition.

- *se hâter de* / to hurry

    Je me hâte de venir chez toi. / I am hurrying to come to your house.

- *offrir de* / to offer

  J'ai offert d'écrire une lettre pour elle. / I offered to write a letter for her.

- *oublier de* / to forget

  J'ai oublié de vous donner la monnaie. / I forgot to give you the change.

- *persuader de* / to persuade

  J'ai persuadé mon père de me prêter quelques euros. / I persuaded my father to lend me a few euros.

- *prendre garde de* / to take care not to

  Prenez garde de tomber. / Be careful not to fall.

- *prier de* / to beg

  Je vous prie d'arrêter. / I beg you to stop.

- *promettre de* / to promise

  J'ai promis de venir chez toi à huit heures. / I promised to come to your place at eight o'clock.

- *refuser de* / to refuse

  Je refuse de le croire. / I refuse to believe it.

- *regretter de* / to regret, be sorry

  Je regrette d'être obligé de vous dire cela. / I am sorry to be obliged to tell you that.

- *remercier de* / to thank

  Je vous remercie d'être venu si vite. / I thank you for coming (having come) so quickly. (Use *remercier de* + infinitive or + abstract noun. Use *remercier pour* + concrete object.)

- *se souvenir de* / to remember

  Tu vois? Je me suis souvenu de venir chez toi. / You see? I remembered to come to your house.

- *tâcher de* / to try

  Tâche de finir tes devoirs avant de sortir. / Try to finish your homework before going out.

- *venir de* / to have just (done something)

  Je viens de manger. / I have just eaten. (I just ate.)

Verb + *à* + Noun + *de* + Infinitive

The model to follow is: *J'ai conseillé à Robert de suivre un cours de français.* / I advised Robert to take a course in French.

- *conseiller à* / to advise

    J'ai conseillé à Jeanne de se marier. / I advised Joan to get married.

- *défendre à* / to forbid

    Mon père défend à mon frère de fumer. / My father forbids my brother to smoke.

- *demander à* / to ask, request

    J'ai demandé à Marie de venir. / I asked Mary to come.

- *dire à* / to say, to tell

    J'ai dit à Charles de venir. / I told Charles to come.

- *interdire à* / to forbid

    Mon père interdit à mon frère de fumer. / My father forbids my brother to smoke.

- *permettre à* / to permit

    J'ai permis à l'étudiant de partir quelques minutes avant la fin de la classe. / I permitted the student to leave a few minutes before the end of class.

- *promettre à* / to promise

    J'ai promis à mon ami d'arriver à l'heure. / I promised my friend to arrive on time.

- *téléphoner à* / to telephone

    J'ai téléphoné à Marcel de venir me voir. / I phoned Marcel to come to see me.

Verb + Other Prepositions

- *commencer par* + infinitive / to begin by + present participle

    La présidente a commencé par discuter des problèmes de la société. / The president began by discussing problems in society.

- *s'entendre avec quelqu'un* / to get along with someone

    Jean s'entend avec Christophe. / John gets along with Christopher.

- *entrer dans* + noun / to enter, go in

    Elle est entrée dans le restaurant. / She went into the restaurant.

- *insister pour* + infinitive / to insist on, upon

    J'insiste pour obtenir tous mes droits. / I insist on obtaining all my rights.

- *se marier avec quelqu'un* / to marry someone

    Elle va se marier avec lui. / She is going to marry him.

- *se mettre en colère* / to become angry, upset

    Monsieur Leduc se met en colère facilement. / Mr. Leduc gets angry easily.

- *se mettre en route* / to start out, set out

    Ils se sont mis en route dès l'aube. / They started out at dawn.

- *remercier pour* + a concrete noun / to thank for

    Je vous remercie pour le joli cadeau. / I thank you for the pretty present. (Remember to use *remercier de* + an abstract noun or + infinitive: *Je vous remercie de votre bonté.* / I thank you for your kindness. *Je vous remercie d'être venue si vite.* / I thank you for coming so quickly.)

Verb + no preposition + Infinitive

The following verbs take *no* preposition and are followed directly by the infinitive.

- *adorer* / to adore, love

    Madame Morin adore naviguer sur Internet. / Mrs. Morin loves to surf the Internet.

- *aimer* / to like

    J'aime lire. / I like to read.

- *aimer mieux* / to prefer

    J'aime mieux rester ici. / I prefer to stay here.

- *aller* / to go

    Je vais faire mes devoirs. / I am going to do my homework.

> **Tip** For the use of **aller** + inf. as a near future tense, see farther on §7.8–4, page 85.

- *compter* / to intend

    Je compte aller en France l'été prochain. / I intend to go to France next summer.

- *croire* / to believe

    Il croit être innocent. / He believes he is innocent.

- *désirer* / to desire, wish

    Je désire prendre une tasse de café. / I wish to have a cup of coffee.

- *devoir* / to have to, ought to

    Je dois faire mes devoirs avant de sortir. / I have to do my homework before going out.

- *écouter* / to listen to

    J'écoute chanter les enfants. / I am listening to the children singing.

- *entendre* / to hear

    J'entends chanter les enfants. / I hear the children singing.

- *espérer* / to hope

    J'espère aller en France. / I hope to go to France.

- *faire* / to cause; to make; to have something done by someone

    Le professeur fait travailler les élèves dans la salle de classe. The teacher has the pupils work in the classroom.

falloir / to be necessary

    Il faut être honnête. / One must be honest.

laisser / to let, allow

    Je vous laisse partir. / I am letting you go.

paraître / to appear, seem

> *Elle paraît être capable.* / She appears to be capable.

penser / to think, plan, intend

> *Je pense aller à Paris.* / I intend to go to Paris.

pouvoir / to be able, can

> *Je peux marcher mieux maintenant.* / I can walk better now.

préférer / to prefer

> *Je préfère manger maintenant.* / I prefer to eat now.

regarder / to look at

> *Je regarde voler les oiseaux.* / I am looking at the birds flying.

savoir / to know, know how

> *Je sais nager.* / I know how to swim.

valoir mieux / to be better

> *Il vaut mieux être honnête.* / It is better to be honest.

vouloir / to want

> *Je veux venir chez vous.* / I want to come to your house.

Verbs That Do Not Require a Preposition

 Tip
In English, there are many "phrasal verbs" that add a preposition or adverb in order to take on a different shade of meaning. However, we often do not need a preposition or adverb to express the same thought in French: to look for / *chercher,* to look at / *regarder.*

- *attendre* / to wait for

> *J'attends l'autobus depuis vingt minutes.* / I have been waiting for the bus for twenty minutes.

- *chercher* / to look for

> *Je cherche mon livre.* / I'm looking for my book.

- *demander* / to ask for

> *Je demande une réponse.* / I am asking for a reply.

- *écouter* / to listen to

    J'écoute la musique. / I am listening to the music.
    J'écoute le professeur. / I am listening to the teacher.

- *envoyer chercher* / to send for

    J'ai envoyé chercher le docteur. / I sent for the doctor.

- *essayer* / to try on

    Elle a essayé une jolie robe. / She tried on a pretty dress.

- *mettre* / to put on

    Elle a mis la robe rouge. / She put on the red dress.

- *payer* / to pay for

    J'ai payé le dîner. / I paid for the dinner.

- *pleurer* / to cry about, cry over

    Elle pleure la perte de son petit chien. / She is crying over the loss of her little dog.

- *regarder* / to look at

    Je regarde le ciel. / I am looking at the sky.

§7.6 COMPLETE CONJUGATION OF AN *AVOIR* VERB

Present participle: *parlant*/ talking, speaking; Past participle: *parlé*/ talked, spoken; Infinitive: *parler*/ to talk, to speak

Present indicative	*je parle, tu parles, il (elle, on) parle; nous parlons, vous parlez, ils (elles) parlent*
	I talk, you talk, he (she, it, one) talks; we talk, you talk, they talk
	OR
	I do talk, etc.
	OR
	I am talking, etc.
Imperfect indicative	*je parlais, tu parlais, il (elle, on) parlait; nous parlions, vous parliez, ils (elles) parlaient*

I was talking, you were talking, he (she, it, one) was talking; we were talking, you were talking, they were talking

OR

I used to talk, etc.

OR

I talked, etc.

Simple past (Past definite)	*je parlai, tu parlas, il (elle, on) parla; nous parlâmes, vous parlâtes, ils (elles) parlèrent*

I talked, you talked, he (she, it, one) talked; we talked, you talked, they talked

OR

I did talk, etc.

Future	*je parlerai, tu parleras, il (elle, on) parlera; nous parlerons, vous parlerez, ils (elles) parleront*

I shall talk, you will talk, he (she, it, one) will talk; we shall talk, you will talk, they will talk

Conditional present	*je parlerais, tu parlerais, il (elle, on) parlerait; nous parlerions, vous parleriez, ils (elles) parleraient*

I would talk, you would talk, he (she, it, one) would talk; we would talk, you would talk, they would talk

Present subjunctive	*que je parle, que tu parles, qu'il (qu'elle, qu'on) parle; que nous parlions, que vous parliez, qu'ils (qu'elles) parlent*

that I may talk, that you may talk, that he (she, it, one) may talk; that we may talk, that you may talk, that they may talk

*Imperfect subjunctive	*que je parlasse, que tu parlasses, qu'il (qu'elle, qu'on) parlât; que nous parlassions, que vous parlassiez, qu'ils (qu'elles) parlassent*
	that I might talk, that you might talk, that he (she, it, one) might talk; that we might talk, that you might talk, that they might talk
Passé composé (Past indefinite)	*j'ai parlé, tu as parlé, il (elle, on) a parlé; nous avons parlé, vous avez parlé, ils (elles) ont parlé*
	I talked, you talked, he (she, it, one) talked; we talked, you talked, they talked
	OR
	I have talked, you have talked, he (she, it, one) has talked; we have talked, you have talked, they have talked
	OR
	I did talk, you did talk, he (she, it, one) did talk; we did talk, you did talk, they did talk
Pluperfect indicative	*j'avais parlé, tu avais parlé, il (elle, on) avait parlé; nous avions parlé, vous aviez parlé, ils (elles) avaient parlé*
	I had talked, you had talked, he (she, it, one) had talked; we had talked, you had talked, they had talked
Past anterior	*j'eus parlé, tu eus parlé, il (elle, on) eut parlé; nous eûmes parlé, vous eûtes parlé, ils (elles) eurent parlé*
	I had talked, you had talked, he (she, it, one) had talked; we had talked, you had talked, they had talked

---

* The imperfect subjunctive is not used much these days. However, you will see it when you read literature.

Future perfect	*j'aurai parlé, tu auras parlé, il (elle, on) aura parlé; nous aurons parlé, vous aurez parlé, ils (elles) auront parlé*
	I shall have talked, you will have talked, he (she, it, one) will have talked; we shall have talked, you will have talked, they will have talked
Conditional perfect	*j'aurais parlé, tu aurais parlé, il (elle, on) aurait parlé; nous aurions parlé, vous auriez parlé, ils (elles) auraient parlé*
	I would have talked, you would have talked, he (she, it, one) would have talked; we would have talked, you would have talked, they would have talked
Past subjunctive	*que j'aie parlé, que tu aies parlé, qu'il (qu'elle, qu'on) ait parlé; que nous ayons parlé, que vous ayez parlé, qu'ils (qu'elles) aient parlé*
	that I may have talked, that you may have talked, that he (she, it, one) may have talked; that we may have talked, that you may have talked, that they may have talked
*Pluperfect subjunctive	*que j'eusse parlé, que tu eusses parlé, qu'il (qu'elle, qu'on) eût parlé; que nous eussions parlé, que vous eussiez parlé, qu'ils (qu'elles) eussent parlé*
	that I might have talked, that you might have talked, that he (she, it, one) might have talked; that we might have talked, that you might have talked, that they might have talked
Imperative	*parle, parlons, parlez*
	talk, let's talk, talk

* The pluperfect subjunctive is not used much these days. However, you may see it when reading literature.

§7.7 COMPLETE CONJUGATION OF AN *ÊTRE* VERB

Present participle: *venant/* coming; Past participle; *venu/* come; Infinitive: *venir/* to come

Present indicative	*je viens, tu viens, il (elle, on) vient; nous venons, vous venez, ils (elles) viennent*

I come, you come, he (she, it, one) comes; we come, you come, they come

OR

I do come, etc.

OR

I am coming, etc.

Imperfect indicative	*je venais, tu venais, il (elle, on) venait; nous venions, vous veniez, ils (elles) venaient*

I was coming, you were coming, he (she, it, one) was coming; we were coming, you were coming, they were coming

OR

I used to come, etc.

OR

I came, etc.

Simple past (Past definite)	*je vins, tu vins, il (elle, on) vint; nous vînmes, vous vîntes, ils (elles) vinrent*

I came, you came, he (she, it, one) came; we came, you came, they came

OR

I did come, etc.

Future	*je viendrai, tu viendras, il (elle, on) viendra; nous viendrons, vous viendrez, ils (elles) viendront*

I shall come, you will come, he (she, it, one) will come; we shall come, you will come, they will come

| Conditional present | *je viendrais, tu viendrais, il (elle, on) viendrait; nous viendrions, vous viendriez, ils (elles) viendraient* |

I would come, you would come, he (she, it, one) would come; we would come, you would come, they would come

| Present subjunctive | *que je vienne, que tu viennes, qu'il (qu'elle, qu'on) vienne; que nous venions, que vous veniez, qu'ils (qu'elles) viennent* |

that I may come, that you may come, that he (she, it, one) may come; that we may come, that you may come, that they may come

| Imperfect subjunctive | *que je vinsse, que tu vinsses, qu'il (qu'elle, qu'on) vînt; que nous vinssions, que vous vinssiez, qu'ils (qu'elles) vinssent* |

that I might come, that you might come, that he (she, it, one) might come; that we might come, that you might come, that they might come

| Passé composé (Past indefinite) | *je suis venu(e), tu es venu(e), il (on) est venu, elle est venue; nous sommes venu(e)s, vous êtes venu(e)(s), ils sont venus, elles sont venues* |

I came, you came, he (she, it one) came; we came, you came, they came

OR

I have come, etc.

OR

I did come, etc.

| Pluperfect indicative | *j'étais venu(e), tu étais venu(e), il, on était venu, elle était venue; nous étions venu(e)s, vous étiez venu(e)(s), ils étaient venus, elles étaient venues* |

I had come, you had come, he (she, it, one) had come; we had come, you had come, they had come

| Past anterior | *je fus venu(e), tu fus venu(e), il (on) fut venu, elle fut venue; nous fûmes venu(e)s, vous fûtes venu(e)(s), ils furent venus, elles furent venues* |

I had come, you had come, he (she, it, one) had come; we had come, you had come, they had come

| Future perfect | *je serai venu(e), tu seras venu(e), il (on) sera venu, elle sera venue; nous serons venu(e)s, vous serez venu(e)(s), ils seront venus, elles seront venues* |

I shall have come, you will have come, he (she, it, one) will have come; we shall have come, you will have come, they will have come

| Conditional perfect | *je serais venu(e), tu serais venu(e), il (on) serait venu, elle serait venue; nous serions venu(e)s, vous seriez venu(e)(s), ils seraient venus, elles seraient venues* |

I would have come, you would have come, he (she, it, one) would have come; we would have come, you would have come, they would have come

| Past subjunctive | *que je sois venu(e), que tu sois venu(e), qu'il (on) soit venu, qu'elle soit venue; que nous* |

soyons venu(e)s, que vous soyez venu(e)(s),
qu'ils soient venus, qu'elles soient venues

that I may have come, that you may have
come, that he (she, it, one) may have come;
that we may have come, that you may have
come, that they may have come

Pluperfect
subjunctive

que je fusse venu(e), que tu fusses venu(e),
qu'il (qu'on) fût venu, qu'elle fût venue; que
nous fussions venu(e)s, que vous fussiez
venu(e)(s), qu'ils fussent venus, qu'elles fussent
venues

that I might have come, that you might have
come, that he (she, it, one) might have
come; that we might have come, that you might have
come, that they might have come

Imperative   *viens, venons, venez*

come, let's come, come

§7.8   TENSES AND MOODS

Beginner Level

§7.8–1   Present Indicative Tense

The *present indicative* is the most frequently used tense in
French and English. It indicates:

• An action or a state of being at the present time.

Je vais à l'école maintenant. / I am going to school now.
Je pense; donc, je suis. / I think; therefore, I am.

• Habitual action.

Je vais à la bibliothèque tous les jours. / I go to the library every
day.

- A general truth, something that is permanently true.

  Deux et deux font quatre. / Two and two are four.
  Voir c'est croire. / Seeing is believing.

- Vividness when talking or writing about past events.

  Marie-Antoinette est condamnée à mort. Elle monte dans la charrette et elle est en route pour la guillotine. / Marie-Antoinette is condemned to die. She gets into the cart and she is on her way to the guillotine.

- A near future.

  Il arrive demain. / He arrives tomorrow.

- An action or state of being that occurred in the past and continues up to the present. In English, this tense is the present perfect, which is formed with the present tense of "to have" plus the past participle of the verb you are using.

  Je suis ici depuis dix minutes. / I have been here for ten minutes. (I am still here at present.)

  This tense is regularly formed as follows:

Drop the *-er* ending of an infinitive like *parler*, and add *-e, -es, -e; -ons, -ez, -ent*.

You then get:
je parle, tu parles, il (elle, on) parle; nous parlons, vous parlez, ils (elles) parlent

---

Drop the *-ir* ending of an infinitive like *finir*, and add *-is, -is, -it; -issons, -issez, -issent*.

You then get:
je finis, tu finis, il (elle, on) finit; nous finissons, vous finissez, ils (elles) finissent

Drop the *-re* ending of an infinitive like *vendre*, and add *-s, -s, —; -ons, -ez, -ent.*

You then get:
je vends, tu vends, il (elle, on) vend; nous vendons, vous vendez, ils (elles) vendent

For the present tense of *avoir* and *être*, see §7.19.

§7.8–2 Imperfect Indicative Tense

The *imperfect indicative* is a past tense. It is used to indicate:

• An action that was going on in the past at the same time as another action.

Il lisait pendant que j'écrivais. / He was reading while I was writing.

• An action that was going on in the past when another action occurred.

Il lisait quand je suis entré. / He was reading when I came in.

• An action that was performed habitually in the past.

Nous allions à la plage tous les jours. / We used to go to the beach every day.

- A description of a mental or physical condition in the past.

> (mental)   *Il était triste quand je l'ai vu.* / He was sad when I saw him.
> (physical)   *Quand ma mère était jeune, elle était belle.* / When my mother was young, she was beautiful.

- An action or state of being that occurred in the past and lasted for a certain length of time prior to another past action.

> *J'attendais l'autobus depuis dix minutes quand il est arrivé.* / I had been waiting for the bus for ten minutes when it arrived.

> This tense is regularly formed as follows:
> For *-er*, *-ir*, and *-re* verbs, take the "*nous*" form in the present indicative tense of the verb you have in mind, drop the first person plural ending (*-ons*), and add the endings *-ais*, *-ais*, *-ait*; *-ions*, *-iez*, *-aient*.

| Tip | The vowel *i* is in each of the six endings and *i* is the first letter of the *imperfect* tense. |

For the imperfect indicative of *avoir* and *être*, see §7.19.

§7.8–3   Simple Past Tense

This past tense is not ordinarily used in conversational French or in informal writing. It is a literary tense — used in formal writing, such as history and literature. The French name of this tense is *le passé simple*. For a summary of the names of verb tenses and moods in French with English equivalents, see page 129.

The simple past tense is regularly formed as follows:
For all -er verbs, drop the -er of the infinitive and add
-ai, -as, -a; -âmes, -âtes, -èrent.
For regular -ir and -re verbs, drop the ending of the
infinitive and add the endings -is, -is, it; -îmes, -îtes, -irent.

> *Il alla en Afrique.* / He went to Africa.
> *Il voyagea en Amérique.* / He traveled to America.
> *Elle fut heureuse.* / She was happy.
> *Elle eut un grand bonheur.* / She had great happiness.

For the past definite of *avoir* and *être*, see §7.19.

§7.8–4   Future Tense

In French and English the *future* tense is used to express an
action or a state of being which will take place at some time in
the future.

> **J'irai en France l'été prochain.* / I will go to France next summer.
> *J'y penserai.* / I will think about it.
> *Je partirai dès qu'il arrivera.* / I will leave as soon as he arrives.
> *Je te dirai tout quand tu seras ici.* / I will tell you all when you are
>   here.

| Tip |

* Instead of using the future tense of **aller** (as in
j'irai), it is correct to use **aller** in the present
tense + infinitive, as in *je vais aller en France
l'été prochain.* / I am going to go to France next
summer.

If the action of the verb you are using is not past or
present and if future time is implied, the future tense is used
when the clause begins with the following conjunctions:
aussitôt que / as soon as, *dès que* / as soon as, *quand* /
when, *lorsque* / when, and *tant que* / as long as.

This tense is regularly formed as follows:
Add the following endings to the whole infinitive: *-ai, -as, -a, -ons, -ez, -ont*. For *-re* verbs you must drop the *e* in *-re* before you add the future endings.

For the future of *avoir* and *être*, see §7.19.

§7.8–5 Conditional Present Tense

The conditional mood is used in French and English to express:

• An action that you would do if something else were possible.

> *Je ferais le travail si j'en avais le temps.* / I would do the work if I had the time.

See also §7.10 for a summary of **si** (if) clauses, on page 95.

• A conditional desire.

> *J'aimerais du thé.* / I would like some tea.

> *Je voudrais du café.* / I would like some coffee.

• An obligation or duty.

> *Je devrais étudier pour l'examen.* / I should study for the examination.

The conditional has two tenses, the present and the past.

The present conditional is regularly formed as follows:
Add the following endings to the whole infinitive: *-ais, -ais, -ait; -ions, -iez, -aient*. For *-re* verbs you must drop the *e* in *-re* before you add the conditional endings. Note that these endings are the same ones you use to form regularly the imperfect indicative. For the conditional of *avoir* and *être*, see §7.19.

Intermediate Level

§7.8–6   Present Subjunctive Tense

The subjunctive mood is used in French much more than in English. It is used in the following ways:

- After a verb that expresses some kind of insistence, preference, or suggestion.

  > *Je préfère qu'il fasse le travail maintenant.* / I prefer that he do the work now.
  > *Le juge exige qu'il soit puni.* / The judge demands that he be punished.

- After a verb that expresses doubt, fear, joy, sorrow, or some other emotion.

  > *Sylvie doute qu'il vienne.* / Sylvia doubts that he is coming.
  > *Je suis heureux qu'il vienne.* / I'm happy that he is coming.
  > *Je regrette qu'il soit malade.* / I'm sorry that he is sick.

- After certain conjunctions.

  > *Elle partira à moins qu'il ne vienne.* / She will leave unless he comes.
  > *Je resterai jusqu'à ce qu'il vienne.* / I will stay until he comes.
  > *Quoiqu'elle soit belle, il ne l'aime pas.* / Although she is beautiful, he does not love her.
  > *Le professeur l'explique pour qu'elle comprenne.* / The teacher is explaining it so that she may understand.

- After certain impersonal expressions that show a need, a doubt, a possibility or an impossibility.

  > *Il est urgent qu'il vienne.* / It is urgent that he come.
  > *Il vaut mieux qu'il vienne.* / It is better that he come.
  > *Il est possible qu'il vienne.* / It is possible that he will come.
  > *Il est douteux qu'il vienne.* / It is doubtful that he will come.

The present subjunctive is regularly formed by dropping the *-ant* ending of the present participle of the verb you are using and adding the endings *-e, -es, -e; -ions, -iez, -ent.*

For the present subjunctive of *avoir* and *être*, see §7.19. See also Subjunctive, §7.15.

§7.8–7 Imperfect Subjunctive Tense

The *imperfect subjunctive* is used in the same ways as the present subjunctive, that is, after certain verbs, conjunctions, and impersonal expressions. The main difference between these two is the time of the action. If present, use the present subjunctive. If the action is related to the past, the imperfect subjunctive is used, provided that the action was not completed.

> *Je voulais qu'il vînt.* / I wanted him to come. (action not
> completed; he did not come while I wanted him to come)

| Tip | Note: The subjunctive of *venir* is used because *vouloir* requires the subjunctive *after* it. In conversational French and informal writing, the imperfect subjunctive is avoided. Use, instead, the present subjunctive. |

> *Je voulais qu'il vienne.* / I wanted him to come.

There is a shortcut to finding the forms of this difficult tense. Go straight to the 3rd person, singular, **passé simple** tense of the verb you have in mind. If the ending is **-a**, as in **parla (parler)**, drop **-a** and add **-asse**, **-asses**, **-ât**; **-assions**, **-assiez**, **-assent**. If the ending is **-it**, as in **finit (finir)** or **vendit (vendre)**, drop **-it** and add **-isse**, **isses**, **-ît**; **-issions**, **issiez**, **issent**.

| Tip | Note: The subjunctive of *comprendre* is used because the conjunction *pour que* requires the subjunctive *after* it. Again, avoid using the imperfect subjunctive in conversation and informal writing. Use, instead, the present subjunctive: *Je le lui expliquais pour qu'elle le comprenne.* |

> If you find the ending **-ut**, as in many irregular **-re** verbs
> **(lire/lut)**, drop **-ut** and add **-usse**, **-usses**, **-ût**; **-ussions**,
> **-ussiez**, **-ussent**. Note the accent mark (ˆ) on **-ât**, **-ît**, **-ût**.

For the imperfect subjunctive of *avoir* and *être*, see §7.19.
See also Subjunctive, §7.15.

§7.8–8 Past Indefinite Tense (Passé Composé)

This past tense is used in conversational French, correspon-
dence, and other informal writing. The past indefinite is used
more and more in literature these days and is taking the place
of the past definite. It is a compound tense because it is
formed with the present indicative of *avoir* or *être* (depending
on which of these two auxiliaries is required to form a
compound tense) plus the past participle. See §7.3 for the
distinction made between verbs conjugated with *avoir* or
être. This is the *passé composé*.

> *Il est allé à l'école.* / He went to school; He did go to school; He
>   has gone to school.
> *J'ai mangé dans ce restaurant de nombreuses fois.* / I have eaten
>   in this restaurant many times.
> *J'ai parlé au garçon.* / I spoke to the boy; I have spoken to the
>   boy; I did speak to the boy.

§7.8–9 Pluperfect Tense

In French and English this tense (also called the *past perfect*)
is used to express an action that happened in the past
before another past action. Since it is used in relation to
another past action, the other past action is expressed in
either the past indefinite or the imperfect indicative in French.
The pluperfect is used in formal writing and literature as well
as in conversational French and informal writing. It is a
compound tense because it is formed with the imperfect

indicative of *avoir* or *être* (depending on which of these two auxiliaries is required to form a compound tense) plus the past participle. See §7.3 for the distinction made between verbs conjugated with *avoir* or *être*.

> *Je me suis rappelé que j'avais oublié de le lui dire.* /
> I remembered that I had forgotten to tell him.

 Tip
Note: It would be incorrect to say: I remembered that I forgot to tell him. The point here is that first I forgot; then I remembered. Both actions are in the past. The action that occurred in the past *before* the other past action is in the pluperfect. And in this example it is "I had forgotten" *(j'avais oublié)*.

> *J'avais étudié la leçon que le professeur a expliquée.* / I had studied the lesson that the teacher explained.

Tip
Note: First I studied the lesson; then the teacher explained it. Both actions are in the past. The action that occurred in the past before the other past action is in the pluperfect. And in this example it is "I had studied" *(j'avais étudié)*.

> *J'étais fatigué ce matin parce que je n'avais pas dormi.* / I was tired this morning because I had not slept.

Advanced Level

§7.8–10 Past Anterior Tense

This tense is similar to the pluperfect indicative. The main difference is that in French it is a literary tense; that is, it is used in formal writing such as history and literature. More and more French writers today use the pluperfect indicative instead of the past anterior. The past anterior is a compound tense and is formed with the *passé simple* of *avoir* or *être* (depending on which of these two auxiliaries is required to form a compound tense) plus the past participle. It is ordinarily introduced by conjunctions of time: *après que, aussitôt que, dès que, lorsque, quand*.

> *Quand il eut tout mangé, il partit.* / When he had eaten everything, he left.

§7.8–11 Future Perfect Tense

In French and English this tense (also called the *future anterior*) is used to express an action that will happen in the future *before* another future action. Since it is used in relation to another future action, the other future action is expressed in the simple future in French. It is used in conversation and informal writing as well as in formal writing and in literature. It is a compound tense because it is formed with the future of *avoir* or *être* (depending on which of these two auxiliaries is required to form a compound tense) plus the past participle of the verb you are using. In English, it is formed by using "will have" plus the past participle of the verb you are using.

> *Elle arrivera demain et j'aurai fini le travail.* / She will arrive tomorrow and I will have finished the work.

Tip	Note: First I will finish the work; then she will arrive. The action that will occur in the future *before* the other future action is in the future anterior.

> *Quand elle arrivera demain, j'aurai fini le travail.* / When she arrives tomorrow, I will have finished the work.

Tip	Note: The idea of future time here is the same as in the preceding example. In English, the present tense is used ("When she arrives . . .") to express a near future. In French, the future is used *(Quand elle arrivera . . .)* because *quand* precedes and the action will take place in the future.

§7.8–12 Conditional Perfect Tense

This is used in French and English to express an action that you would have done if something else had been possible; that is, you would have done something on condition that something else had been possible. It is a compound tense because it is formed with the conditional of *avoir* or *être* plus the past participle of the verb you are using. In English, it is formed by using "would have" plus the past participle.

> *J'aurais fait le travail si j'avais étudié.* / I would have done the work if I had studied.
>
> *J'aurais fait le travail si j'en avais eu le temps.* / I would have done the work if I had had the time.

§7.8–13 Past Subjunctive Tense

This tense is used to express an action that took place in the past in relation to the present. It is like the past indefinite, *(passé composé)* except that the auxiliary verb (avoir or être) is in the present subjunctive. The subjunctive is used because what precedes is a certain verb, conjunction, or impersonal expression. The past subjunctive is also used in relation to a future time when another action will be completed. In French this tense is used in formal writing and in literature as well as in conversation and informal writing. It is a compound tense because it is formed with the present subjunctive of *avoir* or *être* as the auxiliary plus the past participle of the verb you are using.

A past action in relation to the present:

> *Il est possible qu'elle soit partie.* / It is possible that she has left.
> *Je doute qu'il ait fait cela.* / I doubt that he did that.

An action that will take place in the future:

> *Je désire que vous soyez rentré avant dix heures.* / I want you to be back before ten o'clock.

§7.8–14 Pluperfect Subjunctive Tense

This tense (also called the *past perfect*) is used for the same reasons as the imperfect subjunctive—that is, after certain verbs, conjunctions, and impersonal expressions. The main difference between the imperfect and the pluperfect subjunctive is the time of the action in the past. If the action was not completed, the imperfect subjunctive is used; if the action was completed, the pluperfect is used. In French, it is used only in formal writing and literature.

> *Il était possible qu'elle fût partie.* / It was possible that she might have left.

Tip	NOTE: Avoid this tense in French because it is rarely used in conversation and informal writing. You must just be aware of it when you see it in your French readings. Use the past subjunctive instead: *Il était possible qu'elle soit partie.*

§7.8–15 Imperative Mood

The *imperative* mood is used in French and English to express a command or request. It is also used to express an indirect request made in the third person. In both languages it is formed by dropping the subject and using the present tense. There are a few exceptions in both languages when the present subjunctive is used.

Sortez! / Get out! *Asseyez-vous!* / Sit down!
Entrez! / Come in! *Levez-vous!* / Get up!
Soyez à l'heure! / Be on time! (subjunctive used)
Dieu le veuille! / May God grant it! (subjunctive used)
Ainsi soit-il! / So be it! (subjunctive used)

You must drop the final *s* in the second person singular of an *-er* verb. This is done in the affirmative and negative, as in: *Mange!* / Eat! *Ne mange pas!* / Don't eat! However, when the pronouns *y* and *en* are linked to it, the *s* is retained in all regular *-er* verbs and in the verb *aller*. The reason for this is that it makes it easier to link the two elements by pronouncing the *s* as a *z*.

> *Donnes-en!* / Give some!
> *Manges-en!* / Eat some!
> *Vas-y!* / Go there!

INTERMEDIATE AND ADVANCED LEVELS

§7.9 PASSIVE VOICE

When verbs are used in the active voice, which is almost all the time, the subject performs the action. When the *passive* voice is used, the subject of the sentence is not the performer; the action falls on the subject. The agent (the performer) is sometimes expressed, sometimes not, as is done in English. The passive voice, therefore, is composed of the verb in the passive, which is any tense of *être* + the past participle of the verb you are using to indicate the action performed upon the subject. Since *être* is the verb used in the passive voice, the past participle of your other verb must agree with the subject in gender and number.

> *Jacqueline a été reçue à l'université.* / Jacqueline has been accepted at the university.
> *Ce livre est écrit par un auteur célèbre.* / This book is written by a famous author.
> *Cette composition a été écrite par un jeune élève.* / This composition was written by a young student.

There are certain rules you must remember about the passive voice:

- Usually the preposition *de* is used instead of *par* with such verbs as *aimer*, *admirer*, *accompagner*, *apprécier*, *voir*.

Jacqueline est aimée de tout le monde. / Jacqueline is liked (loved) by everyone.

BUT

Nous avons été suivis par un chien perdu. / We were followed by a lost dog.

- Avoid the passive voice if the thought can be expressed in the active voice with the indefinite pronoun *on* as the subject.

    On vend de bonnes choses dans ce magasin. / Good things are sold in this store.
    On parle français ici. / French is spoken here.

- You must avoid using the passive voice with a reflexive verb. Always use a reflexive verb with an active subject.

    Elle s'appelle Jeanne. / She is called Joan.
    Comment se prononce ce mot? / How is this word pronounced?

Sometimes the passive voice is expressed in French with a reflexive verb in the active voice.

Note this example of a reflexive verb with a passive meaning:

    La bibliothèque se situe en face de l'église. / The library is located (situated) opposite the church.

§7.10   *SI* CLAUSE: A SUMMARY

When the Verb in the *Si* clause is in the:	The Verb in the Main or Result Clause is:
present indicative	present indicative, future, or imperative
imperfect indicative	conditional
pluperfect indicative	conditional perfect

- By *si* we mean "if." Sometimes *si* can mean "whether" and in that case, this summary does not apply because there are no restrictions about the tenses. The sequence of tenses with a *si-* clause is the same in English with an "if" clause.

    Si elle arrive, je pars. / If she arrives, I'm leaving.
    Si elle arrive, je partirai. / If she arrives, I will leave.
    Si elle arrive, partez! / If she arrives, leave!

Si Paul étudiait, il aurait de meilleures notes. / If Paul studied, he would have better grades.

Si Georges avait étudié, il aurait eu de bonnes notes. / If George had studied, he would have had good grades.

- Review §7.8–5 about the Conditional, on page 86.

§7.11 SPECIAL USES OF COMMON VERBS

CONNAÎTRE / TO KNOW; TO BE ACQUAINTED WITH; TO MAKE THE ACQUAINTANCE OF

- Present

  Connaissez-vous Mme Vallois? / Do you know Mrs. Vallois?

  Non, je ne la connais pas. / No, I don't know her.

- Conditional

  Mon oncle connaissait New York comme sa poche. / My uncle knew New York like the back of his hand.

- Passé composé

  In the passé composé, *connaître* can mean "to meet" or "to make the acquaintance of."

  Mon père a connu ma mère au Luxembourg. / My father met my mother in Luxembourg.

  See *Savoir* and *Connaître*, page 99.

DEVOIR / TO OWE; OUGHT TO

- Present

  Je dois étudier. / I have to study; I must study; I am supposed to study.

  Il doit être fou! / He must be crazy! He's probably crazy!

  Mon père doit avoir cinquante ans. / My father must be 50 years old.

- Imperfect

  Je devais étudier. / I had to study; I was supposed to study.

  Quand j'étais à l'école, je devais toujours étudier. / When I was in school, I always had to study.

  Ma mère devait avoir cinquante ans quand elle est morte. / My mother was probably 50 years old when she died.

- Future

    Je devrai étudier. / I will have to study.
    Nous devrons faire le travail ce soir. / We will have to do the work this evening.

- Conditional

    Je devrais étudier. / I ought to study. / I should study.
    Vous devriez étudier davantage. / You ought to study more; You should study more.

- Past indefinite

    Je ne suis pas allé(e) au cinéma parce que j'ai dû étudier. / I did not go to the movies because I had to study.
    J'ai dû prendre l'autobus parce qu'il n'y avait pas de train à cette heure-là. / I had to take the bus because there was no train at that hour.
    Robert n'est pas ici. / Robert is not here.
    Il a dû partir. / He must have left; He has probably left; He had to leave.

- Conditional perfect

    J'aurais dû étudier! / I should have studied!
    Vous auriez dû me dire la vérité. / You should have told me the truth.

- With a direct or an indirect object there is still another meaning.

    Je dois de l'argent. / I owe some money.
    Je le lui dois. / I owe it to him (to her).

POUVOIR / TO BE ABLE TO, CAN

Present

    Je ne peux pas sortir aujourd'hui parce que je suis malade. / I cannot (am unable to) go out today because I am sick.
    Est-ce que je peux entrer? Puis-je entrer? / May I come in?
    Madame Marin peut être malade. / Mrs. Marin may be sick.

    This use of *pouvoir* suggests possibility.

Je n'en peux plus. / I can't go on any longer.
This use suggests physical exhaustion.

> *Il se peut.* / It is possible.
> This use as a reflexive verb suggests possibility.

> *Cela ne se peut pas.* / That can't be done.
> This use as a reflexive verb suggests impossibility.

Conditional

> *Pourriez-vous me prêter dix euros?/* Could you lend me ten euros?

Conditional perfect

> *Auriez-vous pu venir chez moi?* / Could you have come to my place?
> *Ils auraient pu rater le train.* / They might have missed the train.

VOULOIR / TO WANT

Present

> *Je veux aller en France.* / I want to go to France.
> *Je veux bien sortir avec vous ce soir.* / I am willing to go out with
> you this evening.
> *Voulez-vous bien vous asseoir?* / Would you be good enough to
> sit down?
> *Que veut dire ce mot?* / What does this word mean?
> *Que voulez-vous dire?* / What do you mean?
> *Qu'est-ce que cela veut dire?* / What does that mean?

- Conditional

> *Je voudrais un café crème, s'il vous plaît.* / I would like coffee
> with cream, please.

- Imperative

> *Veuillez vous asseoir.* / Kindly sit down.
> *Veuillez accepter mes meilleurs sentiments.* / Please accept my
> best regards.

SAVOIR / TO KNOW (a fact)

- Present

> *Je sais la réponse.* / I know the answer.
> *Je sais lire en français.* / I know how to read in French.

- Conditional

  Sauriez-vous où est le docteur? / Would you know where the doctor is?

  Je ne saurais penser à tout! / I can't think of everything!

- Imperative

  Sachons-le bien! / Let's be well aware of it!

  Sachez que votre père vient de mourir. / Be informed that your father has just died.

- Passé composé

  In the passé composé, *savoir* means "to find out."

  J'ai su que le tableau valait mille dollars. / I found out that the painting was worth a thousand dollars.

SAVOIR AND CONNAÎTRE

The main difference between the meaning of these two verbs in the sense of "to know" is that *connaître* means merely to be acquainted with; for example, to be acquainted with a person, a city, a neighborhood, a country, the title of a book, the works of an author.

Savez-vous la réponse? / Do you know the answer?

Savez-vous quelle heure il est? / Do you know what time it is?

Connaissez-vous cette dame? / Do you know this lady?

Connaissez-vous Paris? / Do you know Paris?

Connaissez-vous ce livre? Do you know this book?

ENTENDRE AND COMPRENDRE

The main difference between the meaning of these two verbs is that *entendre* means "to hear" and *comprendre* "to understand." Sometimes *entendre* can mean "to understand" or "to mean."

Entendez-vous la musique? / Do you hear the music?

Comprenez-vous la leçon? / Do you understand the lesson?

"M'entends-tu?!" dit la mère à l'enfant. "Ne fais pas cela!" / "Do you understand me?!" says the mother to the child. "Don't do that!"

Je ne comprends pas M. Grossier parce qu'il parle la bouche pleine. / I do not understand Mr. Grossier because he is talking with his mouth full.

Qu'entendez-vous par là? / What do you mean by that? What are you insinuating by that remark?

Je vous entends, mais je ne vous comprends pas; expliquez-vous, s'il vous plaît. / I hear you, but I don't understand you; explain yourself, please.

QUITTER, PARTIR, SORTIR, AND *LAISSER*

These four verbs all mean "to leave," but note the differences in their uses:

- Use *quitter* when you state a direct object noun or pronoun that could be a person or a place.

    J'ai quitté mes amis devant le théâtre. / I left my friends in front of the theater.

    J'ai quitté la maison à six heures du matin. / I left the house at six in the morning.

- Use *partir* when there is no direct object noun or pronoun.

    Elle est partie tout de suite. / She left immediately.

However, if you use the preposition *de* after *partir*, you may add a direct object, but it would be the object of the preposition *de*, not of the verb *partir*.

    Elle est partie de la maison à six heures du matin. / She left (from) the house at six in the morning.

- Use *sortir*, in the sense of "to go out." With no direct object:

    Elle est sortie il y a une heure. / She went out an hour ago.

However, if you use the preposition *de* after *sortir*, you may add a direct object, but it would be object of the preposition *de*, not of the verb *sortir*.

    Elle est sortie de la maison il y a une heure. / She left (went out of) the house an hour ago.

Note that *sortir* can also be conjugated with *avoir* to form a compound tense, but then the meaning changes because it can take a direct object.

> *Elle a sorti son mouchoir pour se moucher.* / She took out her handkerchief to wipe her nose.
> *Elle a sorti son mouchoir pour moucher son enfant.* / She took out her handkerchief to wipe her child's nose.

- Use *laisser* when you leave behind something that is not stationary; in other words, something movable, for example, books and articles of clothing.

> *J'ai laissé mes livres sur la table dans la cuisine.* / I left my books on the table in the kitchen.
> *J'ai laissé mon imperméable à la maison.* / I left my raincoat at home.

Note that *laisser* also has the meaning "to let, allow a person to do something":

> *J'ai laissé mon ami partir.* / I let (allowed) my friend to leave.

Partir / to leave, go away contains an *a* and so does "away."
Sortir / to go out contains an *o* and so does "out."

FALLOIR

- Falloir is an impersonal verb, which means that it is used only in the third person singular (*il* form) in all the tenses; its primary meaning is "to be necessary." Also, "you have to."

> *Il faut étudier pour avoir de bonnes notes.* / You have to study in order to have good grades.
> *Faut-il le faire tout de suite?* / Is it necessary to do it at once?
> *Oui, il le faut.* / Yes, it is (understood: necessary to do it).

The use of the neuter direct object *le* is needed to show emphasis and to complete the thought.

> *Il faut être honnête.* / It is necessary to be honest.

In the negative:

Il ne faut pas être malhonnête. / One must not be dishonest.

Note that *il faut* in the negative means "one must not."

Il ne faut pas fumer. / One must not smoke.

Proverbe français: *Il ne faut pas condamner sans entendre.* / One must not condemn without a hearing. (No one should be condemned unheard.)

§7.12 OTHER VERBS WITH SPECIAL MEANINGS

arriver / to happen   *Qu'est-ce qui est arrivé?* / What happened?

avoir / to have something the matter   *Qu'est-ce que vous avez?* / What's the matter with you?

entendre dire que / to hear it said that, hear that   *J'entends dire que Robert s'est marié.* / I hear that Robert got married.

entendre parler de / to hear of, about   *J'ai entendu parler d'un grand changement dans l'administration.* / I've heard about a big change in the administration.

envoyer chercher / to send for   *Je vais envoyer chercher le médecin.* / I'm going to send for the doctor.

être à quelqu'un / to belong to someone   *Ce livre est à moi.* / This book belongs to me.

faillir + infinitive   to almost do something   *Le bébé a failli tomber.* / The baby almost fell.

mettre / to put on   *Gisèle a mis sa plus jolie robe.* / Gisèle put on her prettiest dress.

mettre la table / to set the table

profiter de / to take advantage of

rendre visite à / to pay a visit to

venir à / to happen to   *Si nous venons à nous rencontrer, nous pourrons prendre une tasse de café.* / If we happen to meet each other, we can have a cup of coffee.

venir de + infinitive / to have just done something   *Joseph vient de partir.* / Joseph has just left; *Barbara venait de partir quand Françoise est arrivée.* / Barbara had just left when Françoise arrived.

§7.13   INFINITIVES

- In English, an *infinitive* contains the preposition "to" in front of it: "to give," "to finish," "to sell." In French an infinitive has a certain ending. There are three major types of infinitives in French: those that end in *-er* (*donner*); those that end in *-ir* (*finir*); and those that end in *-re* (*vendre*).

- Make an infinitive negative in French by placing *ne pas* in front of it.

    Je vous dis de ne pas sortir. / I am telling you not to go out.

- The infinitive is often used after a verb of perception to express an action that is in progress.

    J'entends quelqu'un chanter. / I hear somebody singing.
    Je vois venir les enfants. / I see the children coming.

    Some common verbs of perception are: *apercevoir* / to perceive, *écouter* / to listen to, *entendre* / to hear, *regarder* / to look at, *sentir* / to feel, *voir* / to see.

- There are certain French verbs that take either the preposition *à* or *de* + infinitive.

    Il commence à pleuvoir. / It is beginning to rain.
    Il a cessé de pleuvoir. / It has stopped raining.

- *Avant de* and *sans* + infinitive

    Sylvie a mangé avant de sortir. / Sylvia ate before going out.
    André est parti sans dire un mot. / Andrew left without saying a word.

Note also the prepositions *afin de* and *pour*.

    Marie est allée en France afin d'améliorer son français. / Mary went to France (in order) to improve her French.
    J'ai mis mon manteau pour sortir. / I put on my coat to go out.

- Use of infinitive instead of a verb form

    Generally speaking, an infinitive is used instead of a verb form if the subject in a sentence is the same for the actions expressed.

    Je veux faire le travail. / I want to do the work.

| Tip | But, if there are two different subjects, you must use a new clause and a new verb form. (Note that the wishes expressed in the following two statements require the subjunctive mood.) |

> *Je veux que vous fassiez le travail.* / I want you to do the work.
> *Je préfère que vous vous couchiez tôt.* / I prefer that you go to bed early.

BUT

> *Préférer* does not require the subjunctive when you are not using the expression *préférer que.*
> *Je préfère me coucher tôt.* / I prefer to go to bed early.

- Past infinitive

In French the past infinitive is expressed by using the infinitive form of *avoir* or *être* + the past participle of the main verb being used.

> *Après avoir quitté la maison, Monsieur et Madame Dubé sont allés au cinéma.* / After leaving the house, Mr. and Mrs. Dubé went to the movies.
> *Après être arrivée, Jeanne a téléphoné à sa mère.* / After arriving, Jeanne telephoned her mother.

§7.14 CAUSATIVE (CAUSAL) *FAIRE*

The construction *faire* + infinitive means to have something done by someone. The causative *faire* can be in any tense, but it must be followed by an infinitive.

Examples with nouns and pronouns as direct and indirect objects:

> *Madame Smith fait travailler ses élèves dans la classe de français.* / Mrs. Smith makes her students work in French class.
>
> In this example, the direct object is the noun *élèves* and it is placed right after the infinitive.

> *Madame Smith les fait travailler dans la classe de français.* /
> Mrs. Smith makes them work (has them work) in French
> class.
>
> In this example, the direct object is the pronoun *les*,
> referring to *les élèves*. It is placed in front of the verb form
> of *faire*, where it logically belongs.

> *Madame Smith fait lire la phrase.* / Mrs. Smith is having the
> sentence read. OR Mrs. Smith has the sentence read.
>
> In this example, the direct object is the noun *phrase* and it
> is placed right after the infinitive, as in the first example.

> *Madame Smith la fait lire.* / Mrs. Smith is having it read.
>
> In this example, the direct object is the pronoun *la*,
> referring to *la phrase*. It is placed in front of the verb form
> of *faire*, where it logically belongs. This is like the second
> example, but here the direct object is a thing. In the other
> two examples, the direct object is a person.

§7.15   SUBJUNCTIVE

The subjunctive is not a tense, but a *mood*, or mode. Usually
when we speak in French or English, we use the indicative
mood, but the subjunctive mood in French must be used in
specific cases. They are:

After Certain Conjunctions Use the Subjunctive

When the following conjunctions introduce a new clause, the
verb in that new clause is usually in the subjunctive mood.

à condition que / on condition that
à moins que / unless
afin que / in order that, so that
attendre que / to wait until
au cas où / in case
bien que / although
de crainte que / for fear that
de peur que / for fear that
de sorte que / so that
en attendant que / until
jusqu'à ce que / until
malgré que / although
pour que / in order that
pourvu que / provided that
quoique / although

> *Je vous explique pour que vous compreniez.* / I am explaining to you so that you will understand.
> *Attendez que je finisse mon dîner.* / Wait until I finish my dinner.
> *Au cas où nous soyons d'accord . . .* / In case we are in agreement . . .

After Indefinite Expressions Use the Subjunctive

où que / wherever
quel que / whatever
qui que / whoever
quoi que / whatever, no matter what

After an Indefinite Antecedent Use the Subjunctive

The subjunctive is needed after an indefinite antecedent because the person or thing desired may possibly not exist; or, if it does exist, you may never find it.

> *Je cherche une personne qui soit honnête.* / I am looking for a person who is honest.
> *Je cherche un appartement qui ne soit pas trop cher.* / I am looking for an apartment that is not too expensive.

Connaissez-vous quelqu'un qui puisse réparer mon ordinateur une fois pour toutes? / Do you know someone who can repair my computer once and for all?

Y a-t-il un élève qui comprenne le subjonctif? / Is there a student who understands the subjunctive?

After a Superlative Expressing an Opinion Use the Subjunctive

 The most common superlatives expressing an opinion are: *le seul* (*la seule*) / the only, *le premier* (*la première*) / the first, *le dernier* (*la dernière*) / the last, *le plus petit* (*la plus petite*) / the smallest, *le plus grand* (*la plus grande*) / the biggest

A mon avis, Marie est la seule étudiante qui comprenne le subjonctif. / In my opinion, Mary is the only student who understands the subjunctive.

Selon mon opinion, Henriette est l'élève la plus jolie que j'aie jamais vue. / According to my opinion, Henrietta is the prettiest pupil I have ever seen.

After *que*, Meaning "Let" or "May," Use the Subjunctive

The subjunctive is required after *que* to express a wish, an order, or a command in the third person singular or plural.

Qu'il parte! / Let him leave!
Que Dieu nous pardonne! / May God forgive us!
Qu'ils s'en aillent! / Let them go away!

After Certain Impersonal Expressions Use the Subjunctive

c'est dommage que / it's a pity that
il est bizarre que / it is odd that
il est bon que / it is good that
il est douteux que / it is doubtful that
il est essentiel que / it is essential that
il est étonnant que / it is astonishing that

il est étrange que / it is strange that
il est heureux que / it is fortunate that
il est honteux que / it is a shame that
il est important que / it is important that
il est impossible que / it is impossible that
il est nécessaire que / it is necessary that
il est possible que / it is possible that
il est regrettable que / it is regrettable that
il est temps que / it is time that
il est urgent que / it is urgent that
il faut que / it is necessary that
il se peut que / it may be that
il semble que / it seems that
il vaut mieux que / it is better that

After Certain Verbs Expressing Doubt, Emotion, or Wishing Use the Subjunctive

aimer que / to like that
aimer mieux que / to prefer that
s'attendre à ce que / to expect that
avoir peur que / to be afraid that
craindre que / to fear that
défendre que / to forbid that
désirer que / to desire that
douter que / to doubt that
empêcher que / to prevent that
s'étonner que / to be astonished that
être bien aise que / to be pleased that
être content que / to be glad that
être désolé que / to be distressed that, sorry that
être étonné que / to be astonished that

être heureux que / to be happy that
être joyeux que / to be joyful that
être ravi que / to be delighted that
être triste que / to be sad that
exiger que / to demand that
se fâcher que / to be angry that
insister que / to insist that
ordonner que / to order that
préférer que / to prefer that
regretter que / to regret that
souhaiter que / to wish that
tenir à ce que / to insist upon
vouloir que / to want

Examples:

J'aimerais que vous restiez ici. / I would like you to stay here.
J'aime mieux que vous restiez ici. / I prefer that you stay here.
Nous nous attendons à ce qu'elle vienne immédiatement. / We expect her to come immediately.
Ta mère est contente que tu sois heureux. / Your mother is glad that you are happy.

After Verbs of Believing and Thinking Use the Subjunctive

Such verbs are *croire*, *penser*, *trouver* (meaning "to think, to have an impression"), and *espérer* when used in the negative or interrogative.

Je ne pense pas qu'il soit coupable. / I don't think that he is guilty.
Croyez-vous qu'il dise la vérité? / Do you believe he is telling the truth?
Trouvez-vous qu'il y ait beaucoup de crimes dans la société d'aujourd'hui? / Do you find (think) that there are many crimes in today's society?

§7.16 SUMMARY OF TENSES AND MOODS

The 7 simple tenses	The 7 compound tenses
Present indicative	Past indefinite (*passé composé*)
Imperfect indicative	Pluperfect indicative
Past definite (Simple past)	Past anterior
Future	Future perfect
Conditional present	Conditional perfect
Present subjunctive	Past subjunctive
Imperfect subjunctive	Pluperfect subjunctive
Imperative or Command	

§7.17 SPELLING IRREGULARITIES OF SOME COMMON VERBS (ORTHOGRAPHICAL CHANGES)

The verbs conjugated here all undergo certain spelling changes in the tenses indicated.*

The subject pronouns have been omitted in order to eliminate repetition and to emphasize the verb forms. They are:

	Singular	**Plural**
1st	*je (j')*	*nous*
2nd	*tu*	*vous*
3rd	*il, elle, on*	*ils, elles*

---

* Review §1., **Guide to Pronouncing French Sounds,** pages 1–4, to understand why some verb forms change in spelling.

PRESENT INDICATIVE

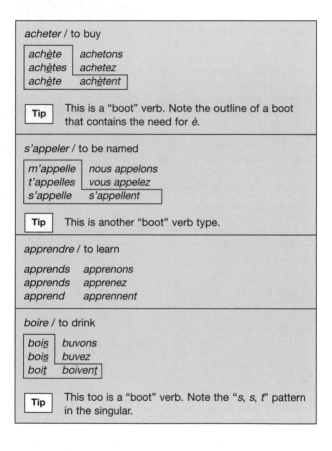

acheter / to buy

achète	achetons
achètes	achetez
achète	achètent

Tip This is a "boot" verb. Note the outline of a boot that contains the need for *è*.

s'appeler / to be named

m'appelle	nous appelons
t'appelles	vous appelez
s'appelle	s'appellent

Tip This is another "boot" verb type.

apprendre / to learn

apprends	apprenons
apprends	apprenez
apprend	apprennent

boire / to drink

bois	buvons
bois	buvez
boit	boivent

Tip This too is a "boot" verb. Note the "*s, s, t*" pattern in the singular.

commencer / to begin, start

commence	*commençons*
commences	*commencez*
commence	*commencent*

comprendre / to understand (like *prendre,* page 116; add *com* at the beginning of *prendre*)

conduire / to drive; to lead

conduis	*conduisons*
conduis	*conduisez*
conduit	*conduisent*

connaître / to know, to be acquainted with

connais	*connaissons*
connais	*connaissez*
connaît	*connaissent*

courir / to run

cours	*courons*
cours	*courez*
court	*courent*

croire / to believe

crois	*croyons*
crois	*croyez*
croit	*croient*

devenir / to become

deviens	*devenons*
deviens	*devenez*
devient	*deviennent*

devoir / to owe; to have to

dois	devons
dois	devez
doit	doivent

dire / to say; to tell

dis	disons
dis	dites
dit	disent

dormir / to sleep

dors	dormons
dors	dormez
dort	dorment

écrire / to write

écris	écrivons
écris	écrivez
écrit	écrivent

envoyer / to send

envoie	envoyons
envoies	envoyez
envoie	envoient

espérer / to hope

espère	espérons
espères	espérez
espère	espèrent

falloir / to be necessary

il faut

se lever / to get up

me lève	nous levons
te lèves	vous levez
se lève	se lèvent

lire / to read

lis	lisons
lis	lisez
lit	lisent

manger / to eat

mange	mangeons
manges	mangez
mange	mangent

mettre / to place, put; to put on

mets	mettons
mets	mettez
met	mettent

mourir / to die

meurs	mourons
meurs	mourez
meurt	meurent

nager / to swim

nage	nageons
nages	nagez
nage	nagent

naître / to be born

nais	naissons
nais	naissez
naît	naissent

offrir / to offer

offre	offrons
offres	offrez
offre	offrent

ouvrir / to open

ouvre	ouvrons
ouvres	ouvrez
ouvre	ouvrent

partir / to leave

pars	partons
pars	partez
part	partent

pleuvoir / to rain

il pleut

pouvoir / to be able, can

peux OR *puis*	pouvons
peux	pouvez
peut	peuvent

Note: In the affirmative, it is most common to say "Je peux." In the inverted interrogative, you should say "Puis-je?"

préférer / to prefer

préfère	préférons
préfères	préférez
préfère	préfèrent

prendre / to take

prends	prenons
prends	prenez
prend	prennent

protéger / to protect

protège	protégeons
protèges	protégez
protège	protègent

recevoir / to receive

reçois	recevons
reçois	recevez
reçoit	reçoivent

revenir / to return, come back (like *venir*, page 117; add *re-* at the beginning of *venir*)

rire / to laugh

ris	rions
ris	riez
rit	rient

savoir / to know (a fact)

sais	savons
sais	savez
sait	savent

servir / to serve

sers	servons
sers	servez
sert	servent

sortir / to go out; to leave

sors	*sortons*
sors	*sortez*
sort	*sortent*

tenir / to hold

tiens	*tenons*
tiens	*tenez*
tient	*tiennent*

venir / to come

viens	*venons*
viens	*venez*
vient	*viennent*

vivre / to live

vis	*vivons*
vis	*vivez*
vit	*vivent*

voir / to see

vois	*voyons*
vois	*voyez*
voit	*voient*

vouloir / to want

veux	*voulons*
veux	*voulez*
veut	*veulent*

voyager / to travel

voyage	*voyageons*
voyages	*voyagez*
voyage	*voyagent*

IMPERFECT INDICATIVE

---

apprendre / to learn

apprenais	apprenions
apprenais	appreniez
apprenait	apprenaient

---

boire / to drink

buvais	buvions
buvais	buviez
buvait	buvaient

---

commencer / to begin, to start

commençais	commencions
commençais	commenciez
commençait	commençaient

---

comprendre / to understand (like *prendre*, page 121; add *com* at the beginning of *prendre*)

---

conduire / to drive; to lead

conduisais	conduisions
conduisais	conduisiez
conduisait	conduisaient

---

connaître / to know, be acquainted with

connaissais	connaissions
connaissais	connaissiez
connaissait	connaissaient

---

courir / to run

courais	courions
courais	couriez
courait	couraient

croire / to believe

croyais	croyions
croyais	croyiez
croyait	croyaient

devenir / to become

devenais	devenions
devenais	deveniez
devenait	devenaient

devoir / to owe; to have to

devais	devions
devais	deviez
devait	devaient

dire / to say; to tell

disais	disions
disais	disiez
disait	disaient

dormir / to sleep

dormais	dormions
dormais	dormiez
dormait	dormaient

écrire / to write

écrivais	écrivions
écrivais	écriviez
écrivait	écrivaient

falloir / to be necessary

il fallait

lire / to read

lisais	lisions
lisais	lisiez
lisait	lisaient

manger / to eat

mang*e*ais	mangions
mang*e*ais	mangiez
mang*e*ait	mang*e*aient

mourir / to die

mourais	mourions
mourais	mouriez
mourait	mouraient

nager / to swim

nag*e*ais	nagions
nag*e*ais	nagiez
nag*e*ait	nag*e*aient

naître / to be born

naissais	naissions
naissais	naissiez
naissait	naissaient

offrir / to offer

offrais	offrions
offrais	offriez
offrait	offraient

ouvrir / to open

ouvrais	ouvrions
ouvrais	ouvriez
ouvrait	ouvraient

partir / to leave

partais	*partions*
partais	*partiez*
partait	*partaient*

pleuvoir / to rain

il pleuvait

prendre / to take

prenais	*prenions*
prenais	*preniez*
prenait	*prenaient*

protéger / to protect

protégeais	*protégions*
protégeais	*protégiez*
protégeait	*protégeaient*

revenir / to return, to come back (like *venir*, page 122; add *re* at the beginning of *venir*)

rire / to laugh

riais	*riions*
riais	*riiez*
riait	*riaient*

savoir / to know (a fact)

savais	*savions*
savais	*saviez*
savait	*savaient*

servir / to serve

servais	*servions*
servais	*serviez*
servait	*servaient*

sortir / to go out; to leave

sortais	*sortions*
sortais	*sortiez*
sortait	*sortaient*

tenir / to hold

tenais	*tenions*
tenais	*teniez*
tenait	*tenaient*

venir / to come

venais	*venions*
venais	*veniez*
venait	*venaient*

vivre / to live

vivais	*vivions*
vivais	*viviez*
vivait	*vivaient*

voir / to see

voyais	*voyions*
voyais	*voyiez*
voyait	*voyaient*

vouloir / to want

voulais	*voulions*
voulais	*vouliez*
voulait	*voulaient*

voyager / to travel

voyageais	*voyagions*
voyageais	*voyagiez*
voyageait	*voyageaient*

§7.18   BASIC NEGATIONS OF VERBS

The common negations of verbs are *ne* + verb + any of the following:

aucun, aucune / no, not one, not any

> *Je n'ai aucun livre.* / I have no book.
> *Robert n'a aucune amie.* / Robert has no girlfriend.

guère / hardly, scarcely

> *Paul ne parle guère.* / Paul hardly (scarcely) talks.

jamais / never

> *Jean n'étudie jamais.* / John never studies.

ni . . . ni / neither . . . nor

> *Je n'ai ni argent ni billet.* / I have neither money nor tickets.

nul, nulle / no, not any

> *Je n'en ai nul besoin.* / I have no need of it.
> *Je ne vais nulle part.* / I'm not going anywhere.

pas / not

> *Je n'ai pas de papier.* / I haven't any paper.

pas du tout / not at all

> *Je ne comprends pas du tout.* / I do not understand at all.

personne / nobody, no one, not anybody

> *Je ne vois personne.* / I don't see anybody. I see no one.

plus / any longer, no more, not anymore

> *Mon père ne travaille plus.* / My father doesn't work anymore.

point / not at all

> *Cet enfant n'a point d'argent.* / This child has no money at all.

que / only, but only

> *Je n'ai que deux euros.* / I have (but) only two euros.

rien / nothing

> *Je n'ai rien sur moi.* / I have nothing on me.

Tip	Note that all these negations require *ne* in front of the main verb. Also note that *aucun, aucune, nul, nulle, personne, rien* can be used as subjects and you still need to use *ne* in front of the verb.

> *Personne n'entend le bruit.* / Nobody hears the noise.
> *Rien n'est jamais parfait.* / Nothing is ever perfect.

Tip	*Une devinette* / a riddle

> *J'ai des yeux mais je n'ai pas de paupières et je vis dans l'eau. Qui suis-je?* / I have eyes but I don't have eyelids and I live in the water. Who am I?

> *un poisson* / a fish

§7.19   FOUR CONJUGATED VERBS

The following irregular verbs – *aller, avoir, être,* and *faire* – have been fully conjugated in all their tenses because they are so frequently used.

aller / **to go**
Present participle: *allant*   **Past participle:** *allé(e)(s)*

The Seven Simple Tenses		The Seven Compound Tenses	
Singular	**Plural**	**Singular**	**Plural**
Present indicative		Past indefinite (passé composé)	
vais	*allons*	*suis allé(e)*	*sommes allé(e)s*
vas	*allez*	*es allé(e)*	*êtes allé(e)(s)*
va	*vont*	*est allé(e)*	*sont allé(e)s*
Imperfect indicative		Pluperfect OR Past perfect indicative	
allais	*allions*	*étais allé(e)*	*étions allé(e)s*
allais	*alliez*	*étais allé(e)*	*étiez allé(e)(s)*
allait	*allaient*	*était allé(e)*	*étaient allé(e)s*
Simple past		Past anterior	
allai	*allâmes*	*fus allé(e)*	*fûmes allé(e)s*
allas	*allâtes*	*fus allé(e)*	*fûtes allé(e)(s)*
alla	*allèrent*	*fut allé(e)*	*furent allé(e)s*
Future		Future perfect OR Future anterior	
irai	*irons*	*serai allé(e)*	*serons allé(e)s*
iras	*irez*	*seras allé(e)*	*serez allé(e)(s)*
ira	*iront*	*sera allé(e)*	*seront allé(e)s*
Conditional		Conditional perfect	
irais	*irions*	*serais allé(e)*	*serions allé(e)s*
irais	*iriez*	*serais allé(e)*	*seriez allé(e)(s)*
irait	*iraient*	*serait allé(e)*	*seraient allé(e)s*
Present subjunctive		Past subjunctive	
aille	*allions*	*sois allé(e)*	*soyons allé(e)s*
ailles	*alliez*	*sois allé(e)*	*soyez allé(e)(s)*
aille	*aillent*	*soit allé(e)*	*soient allé(e)s*
Imperfect subjunctive		Pluperfect OR Past perfect subjunctive	
allasse	*allassions*	*fusse allé(e)*	*fussions allé(e)s*
allasses	*allassiez*	*fusses allé(e)*	*fussiez allé(e)(s)*
allât	*allassent*	*fût allé(e)*	*fussent allé(e)s*

Imperative OR Command
va
allons
allez

avoir / **to have**
Present participle: *ayant*   **Past participle:** *eu*

The Seven Simple Tenses		The Seven Compound Tenses	
Singular	**Plural**	**Singular**	**Plural**
Present indicative		Past indefinite (passé composé)	
ai	*avons*	*ai eu*	*avons eu*
as	*avez*	*as eu*	*avez eu*
a	*ont*	*a eu*	*ont eu*
Imperfect indicative		Pluperfect OR Past perfect indicative	
avais	*avions*	*avais eu*	*avions eu*
avais	*aviez*	*avais eu*	*aviez eu*
avait	*avaient*	*avait eu*	*avaient eu*
Simple past		Past anterior	
eus	*eûmes*	*eus eu*	*eûmes eu*
eus	*eûtes*	*eus eu*	*eûtes eu*
eut	*eurent*	*eut eu*	*eurent eu*
Future		Future perfect OR Future anterior	
aurai	*aurons*	*aurai eu*	*aurons eu*
auras	*aurez*	*auras eu*	*aurez eu*
aura	*auront*	*aura eu*	*auront eu*
Conditional		Conditional perfect	
aurais	*aurions*	*aurais eu*	*aurions eu*
aurais	*auriez*	*aurais eu*	*auriez eu*
aurait	*auraient*	*aurait eu*	*auraient eu*
Present subjunctive		Past subjunctive	
aie	*ayons*	*aie eu*	*ayons eu*
aies	*ayez*	*aies eu*	*ayez eu*
ait	*aient*	*ait eu*	*aient eu*
Imperfect subjunctive		Pluperfect OR Past perfect subjunctive	
eusse	*eussions*	*eusse eu*	*eussions eu*
eusses	*eussiez*	*eusses eu*	*eussiez eu*
eût	*eussent*	*eût eu*	*eussent eu*

Imperative OR Command
aie
ayons
ayez

être / to be

Present participle: *étant*   **Past participle:** *été*

The Seven Simple Tenses		The Seven Compound Tenses	
Singular	**Plural**	**Singular**	**Plural**
Present indicative		Past indefinite (passé composé)	
suis	sommes	ai été	avons été
es	êtes	as été	avez été
est	sont	a été	ont été
Imperfect indicative		Pluperfect OR Past perfect indicative	
étais	étions	avais été	avions été
étais	étiez	avais été	aviez été
était	étaient	avait été	avaient été
Simple past		Past anterior	
fus	fûmes	eus été	eûmes été
fus	fûtes	eus été	eûtes été
fut	furent	eut été	eurent été
Future		Future perfect OR Future anterior	
serai	serons	aurai été	aurons été
seras	serez	auras été	aurez été
sera	seront	aura été	auront été
Conditional		Conditional perfect	
serais	serions	aurais été	aurions été
serais	seriez	aurais été	auriez été
serait	seraient	aurait été	auraient été
Present subjunctive		Past subjunctive	
sois	soyons	aie été	ayons été
sois	soyez	aies été	ayez été
soit	soient	ait été	aient été
Imperfect subjunctive		Pluperfect OR Past perfect subjunctive	
fusse	fussions	eusse été	eussions été
fusses	fussiez	eusses été	eussiez été
fût	fussent	eût été	eussent été

Imperative OR Command

sois

soyons

soyez

faire / **to do, to make**
Present participle: *faisant*   **Past participle:** *fait*

The Seven Simple Tenses		The Seven Compound Tenses	
Singular	**Plural**	**Singular**	**Plural**
Present indicative		Past indefinite (passé composé)	
fais	*faisons*	*ai fait*	*avons fait*
fais	*faites*	*as fait*	*avez fait*
fait	*font*	*a fait*	*ont fait*
Imperfect indicative		Pluperfect OR Past perfect indicative	
faisais	*faisions*	*avais fait*	*avions fait*
faisais	*faisiez*	*avais fait*	*aviez fait*
faisait	*faisaient*	*avait fait*	*avaient fait*
Simple past		Past anterior	
fis	*fîmes*	*eus fait*	*eûmes fait*
fis	*fîtes*	*eus fait*	*eûtes fait*
fit	*firent*	*eut fait*	*eurent fait*
Future		Future perfect OR Future anterior	
ferai	*ferons*	*aurai fait*	*aurons fait*
feras	*ferez*	*auras fait*	*aurez fait*
fera	*feront*	*aura fait*	*auront fait*
Conditional		Conditional perfect	
ferais	*ferions*	*aurais fait*	*aurions fait*
ferais	*feriez*	*aurais fait*	*auriez fait*
ferait	*feraient*	*aurait fait*	*auraient fait*
Present subjunctive		Past subjunctive	
fasse	*fassions*	*aie fait*	*ayons fait*
fasses	*fassiez*	*aies fait*	*ayez fait*
fasse	*fassent*	*ait fait*	*aient fait*
Imperfect subjunctive		Pluperfect OR Past perfect subjunctive	
fisse	*fissions*	*eusse fait*	*eussions fait*
fisses	*fissiez*	*eusses fait*	*eussiez fait*
fît	*fissent*	*eût fait*	*eussent fait*

Imperative OR Command
fais
faisons
faites

Summary of verb tenses and moods in French with English equivalent

Les Sept Temps Simples *The Seven Simple Tenses*		Les Sept Temps Composés *The Seven Compound Tenses*	
Tense No.	Tense Name	Tense No.	Tense Name
1	**Présent de l'indicatif** *Present indicative*	8	**Passé composé** *Past indefinite*
2	**Imparfait de l'indicatif** *Imperfect indicative*	9	**Plus-que-parfait de l'indicatif** *Pluperfect indicative*
3	**Passé simple** *Past definite or Simple past*	10	**Passé antérieur** *Past anterior*
4	**Futur** *Future*	11	**Futur antérieur** *Future perfect*
5	**Conditionnel** *Conditional*	12	**Conditionnel passé** *Conditional perfect*
6	**Présent du subjonctif** *Present subjunctive*	13	**Passé du subjonctif** *Past subjunctive*
7	**Imparfait du subjonctif** *Imperfect subjunctive*	14	**Plus-que-parfait du subjonctif** *Pluperfect subjunctive*

The imperative is not a tense; it is a mood.

§8.

Adverbs

DEFINITION

An *adverb* is a word that modifies a verb, an adjective, or
another adverb.

§8.1 FORMATION

Many French adverbs are not formed from another word, for
example: *bien, mal, vite, combien, comment, pourquoi, où.*

There are many other adverbs that are formed from
another word. The usual way is to add the suffix *-ment* to the
masculine singular form of an adjective whose last letter is a
vowel; for example: *probable, probablement; poli, poliment;
vrai, vraiment.*

The suffix *-ment* is added to the feminine singular form if
the masculine singular ends in a consonant; for example:
*affreux, affreuse, affreusement; seul, seule, seulement; amer,
amère, amèrement; franc, franche, franchement.*

The ending *-ment* is equivalent to the English ending "-ly":
lent, lente, lentement / slow, slowly.

Some adjectives that end in *-ant* or *-ent* become
adverbs by changing *-ant* to *-amment* and *-ent* to *-emment*:
*innocent, innocemment; constant, constamment; récent,
récemment.*

Some adverbs take *é* instead of *e* before adding *-ment*:
*profond, profondément; confus, confusément; précis,
précisément.*

The adjective *gentil* becomes *gentiment* as an adverb and
bref becomes *brièvement.*

§8.2   POSITION

1. *David aime beaucoup les chocolats.*
2. *Paulette a parlé distinctement.*
3. *Julie a bien parlé.*

- In French, an adverb ordinarily follows the simple verb it modifies, as in the first model sentence above.
- If a verb is compound, as in the *past indefinite* (sentence 2), the adverb generally follows the past participle if it is a long adverb. The adverb *distinctement* is long. Some exceptions: *certainement, complètement,* and *probablement* are usually placed between the helping verb and the past participle: *Elle est probablement partie. Il a complètement fini le travail.*
- If a verb is compound, as in the *past indefinite* (sentence 3), short common adverbs (like *beaucoup, bien, déjà, encore, mal, mieux, souvent, toujours*) ordinarily precede the past participle; in other words, they may be placed between the helping verb and the past participle.
- For emphasis, an adverb may be placed at the beginning of a sentence: *Malheureusement, Suzanne est déjà partie.*

§8.3   TYPES

§8.3–1   Interrogative Adverbs

Some common interrogative adverbs are *comment, combien, pourquoi, quand, où.*

Examples:

Comment allez-vous? Combien coûte ce livre? Pourquoi partez-vous? Quand arriverez-vous? Où allez-vous?

§8.3–2 Adverbs of Quantity

Some adverbial expressions of quantity are *beaucoup de,
assez de, peu de, trop de, plus de*. With these, no article is
used: *peu de sucre, beaucoup de travail, assez de temps, trop
de lait, combien d'argent.*

§8.3–3 Comparative and Superlative Adverbs

Adverb	Comparative	Superlative
vite / quickly	*plus vite (que)* / more quickly (than) faster (than)	*le plus vite* / (the) most quickly, (the) fastest
	moins vite (que) / less quickly (than)	*le moins vite* / (the) least quickly
	aussi vite (que) / as quickly (as), as fast (as)	

Examples:

Arlette parle plus vite que Marie-France. / Arlette speaks faster than
   Marie-France.
Madame Legrange parle moins vite que Madame Duval. / Madame
   Legrange speaks less quickly than Madame Duval.
Monsieur Bernard parle aussi vite que Monsieur Claude. / Monsieur
   Bernard speaks as fast as Monsieur Claude.
*Madame Durocher parle le plus vite tandis que Madame
   Milot parle le moins vite.* / Madame Durocher speaks the fastest
   whereas Madame Milot speaks the least fast (the slowest).
Aussi . . . que should become *si...que* in a negative sentence.
   However, native speakers do not always make this change.
   See also §5.4–5.

Examples:

Justin ne parle pas si vite que Justine. / Justin does not talk as fast as Justine.

Irregular Comparative and Superlative Adverb

Adverb	Comparative	Superlative
bien / well	*mieux* / better	*le mieux* / best, the best
beaucoup / much	*plus* / more	*le plus* / most, the most
mal / badly	*plus mal* / worse *pis* / worse	*le plus mal* / worst, the worst *le moins bien* / the worst *le pis* / worst, the worst
peu / little	*moins* / less	*le moins* / least, the least

Examples:

Pierre travaille bien, Henri travaille mieux que Robert et Georges travaille le mieux.
Marie étudie beaucoup, Paulette étudie plus que Marie, et Henriette étudie le plus.

§8.4 *OUI* AND *SI*

Ordinarily, *oui* is used to mean "yes." However, *si* can also be used to mean "yes" in response to a question in the negative.

Examples:

Aimez-vous le français?—Oui, j'aime le français.
N'aimez-vous pas le français?—Si, j'aime le français.

 Tip *Une scie* (pronounced like the English "see") is a carpenter's "saw."

§9.

Prepositions—Special Uses

§9.1 *DANS* AND *EN* + A LENGTH OF TIME

The prepositions *dans* and *en* both mean "in," but each is
used in a different sense.

    Dans + a length of time indicates that something will hap-
pen *at the end* of that length of time.

> *Le docteur va venir dans une demi-heure.* / The doctor will come
> in a half-hour (*i.e.,* at the end of a half-hour).

    Dans and a duration of time can be at the beginning
of the sentence or at the end of it and future time is
ordinarily implied.

    En + a length of time indicates that something
happened or will happen at any time *within* that length
of time.

Examples:
> *Robert a fait cela en une heure.* / Robert did that in (within) an (one)
> hour.
> *Robert fera cela en une heure.* / Robert will do that in (within) an
> (one) hour.

BUT

> *Robert fera cela dans une heure.* / Robert will do that in (at the end
> of) an (one) hour.

§9.2 *ENVERS* AND *VERS*

Envers is used in a figurative sense in the meaning of "with
regard to" someone, "with respect to" someone, "for"
someone, or "for" something.

Examples:
> *Je montre beaucoup de respect envers les vieilles personnes.* /
> I show a lot of respect toward old persons.

134

Je ne montre aucun respect envers un criminel. / I show no respect toward a criminal.

Vers also means "toward," but is used in the physical sense (in the direction of) as well as in the figurative sense.

Examples:

Pourquoi allez-vous vers la porte? / Why are you going toward the door?

Je vais partir vers trois heures. / I am going to leave toward (around) three o'clock.

§9.3 *PENDANT*

IN THE PRESENT TENSE

Combien de temps étudiez-vous chaque soir? / How long do you study every evening?

J'étudie une heure chaque soir. / I study one hour each night. OR *J'étudie pendant une heure chaque soir.* / I study for one hour each night.

IN THE PAST INDEFINITE

Combien de temps êtes-vous resté(e) à Paris? / How long did you stay in Paris?

Je suis resté(e) à Paris deux semaines. / I stayed in Paris two weeks. OR *Je suis resté(e) à Paris pendant deux semaines.* / I stayed in Paris for two weeks.

IN THE FUTURE

Combien de temps resterez-vous à Paris? / How long will you stay in Paris?

J'y resterai pendant deux semaines. / I will stay there for two weeks. OR *J'y resterai deux semaines.* / I will stay there two weeks.

§10.

Conjunctions

§10.1 DEFINITION

A conjunction is a word that connects words, phrases, clauses, or sentences, such as *et* / and, *mais* / but, *ou* / or, *parce que* / because. The following is a list of the most common conjunctions.

§10.2 BASIC CONJUNCTIONS

Review §7.15, the Subjunctive after Certain Conjunctions.

à moins que / unless
afin que / in order that, so that
aussitôt que / as soon as
avant que / before
bien que / although
car / for
comme / as, since
de crainte que / for fear that
de peur que / for fear that
de sorte que / so that, in such a way that
depuis que / since
dès que / as soon as
donc / therefore, consequently
en même temps que / at the same time as
et / and
jusqu'à ce que / until
lorsque / when, at the time when
maintenant que / now that
mais / but
ou / or
parce que / because
pendant le temps que / while
pendant que / while
pour que / in order that
pourvu que / provided that

puisque / since
quand / when
que / that
quoi que / whatever, no matter what
quoique / although
si / if
tandis que / while, whereas

 Pronounce the final *c* in *donc* as a *k* when it means consequently (therefore).
Je pense; donc, je suis, I think; therefore, I am.

Special Topics

§11.

Order of Elements in French Sentences

§11.1 REVIEW OF NEGATIVE CONSTRUCTIONS

Please review §7.18 before studying the following sections.

§11.2 DECLARATIVE SENTENCE WITH A VERB IN A SIMPLE TENSE (*e.g.,* PRESENT)

$$\text{SUBJECT} \rightarrow \textbf{\textit{ne (n')}} + \begin{Bmatrix} me\ (m') \\ te\ (t') \\ se\ (s') \\ nous \\ vous \end{Bmatrix} \text{OR} \begin{Bmatrix} le \\ la \\ l' \\ les \end{Bmatrix} \text{AND/OR} \begin{Bmatrix} lui \\ leur \end{Bmatrix}$$
$$\text{OR } y + en + \textbf{VERB} \rightarrow \textbf{\textit{pas}}$$

Examples:
Il ne me les donne pas. / He is not giving them to me.
Je ne le leur donne pas. / I am not giving it to them.
Il n'y en a pas. / There aren't any of them.

§11.3 DECLARATIVE SENTENCE WITH A VERB IN A COMPOUND TENSE (*e.g., PASSÉ COMPOSÉ*)

$$\textbf{SUBJECT} \rightarrow \textbf{\textit{ne (n')}} + \begin{Bmatrix} me\ (m') \\ te\ (t') \\ se\ (s') \\ nous \\ vous \end{Bmatrix} \text{OR} \begin{Bmatrix} le \\ la \\ l' \\ les \end{Bmatrix} \text{AND/OR} \begin{Bmatrix} lui \\ leur \end{Bmatrix}$$

OR *y* + *en* + **VERB** → ***pas*** + past participle (auxiliary verb *avoir* or *être* in a simple tense)

Examples:

Yvonne ne s'est pas lavée. / Yvonne did not wash herself.
Il ne m'en a pas envoyé. / He did not send any of them to me.
Je ne le lui ai pas donné. / I did not give it to him (to her).
Nous ne vous les avons pas données. / We have not given them to you.
Ils ne s'en sont pas allés. / They did not go away.

§11.4 AFFIRMATIVE IMPERATIVE SENTENCE

$$\text{VERB} + \begin{Bmatrix} le \\ la \\ l' \\ les \end{Bmatrix} \text{OR} \begin{Bmatrix} moi\ (m') \\ toi\ (t') \\ nous \\ vous \end{Bmatrix} \text{AND/OR} \begin{Bmatrix} lui \\ leur \end{Bmatrix} \text{OR } y + en$$

Examples:

Donnez-les-leur. / Give them to them.
Assieds-toi. / Sit down.
Allez-vous-en! / Go away!
Apportez-le-moi! / Bring it to me!
Donnez-m'en! / Give me some!
Allez-y! / Go to it! Go there!

§11.5   NEGATIVE IMPERATIVE SENTENCE

$$\text{Ne (N')} + \begin{Bmatrix} me\ (m') \\ te\ (t') \\ nous \\ vous \end{Bmatrix} \text{OR} \begin{Bmatrix} le \\ la \\ l' \\ les \end{Bmatrix} \text{OR} \begin{Bmatrix} lui \\ leur \end{Bmatrix} \text{OR } y + en + \textbf{VERB} \rightarrow \textit{pas}$$

Examples:
Ne l'y mettez pas. / Do not put it in it. Do not put it there.
Ne les leur donnez pas. / Do not give them to them.
Ne t'assieds pas! / Don't sit down!
Ne vous en allez pas! / Don't go away!

Tip

Object pronouns fall in the right order if you alphabetize them!

$$\begin{rcases} la \\ le \\ les \end{rcases} \begin{array}{l} +\ leur \\ +\ lui \\ + \end{array}$$

The order is always the same, whether before or after a verb or before an infinitive.

Idioms and Idiomatic Expressions

§12.1   SPECIAL USES

Depuis

• With the present indicative tense

When an action of some sort began in the past and is still going on in the present, use the present tense with *depuis* + the length of time.

> *Je travaille dans ce bureau depuis trois ans.* / I have been working in this office for three years.

 Tip   Use *depuis combien de temps* + the present indicative of the verb to ask how long one has been + verb: *Depuis combien de temps travaillez-vous dans ce bureau?* / How long have you been working in this office? *Je travaille dans ce bureau depuis un an.* / I have been working in this office for one year.

• With the imperfect indicative tense

When an action of some sort began in the past and contin-ued up to another point in the past that you are telling about, use the imperfect indicative tense with depuis + the length of time:

> *J'attendais l'autobus depuis vingt minutes quand il est arrivé.* / I had been waiting for the bus for twenty minutes when it arrived.

• In a question

> *Depuis combien de temps attendez-vous l'autobus?* / How long have you been waiting for the bus?
>
> *J'attends l'autobus depuis vingt minutes.* / I have been waiting for the bus for twenty minutes.

| Tip | Note: When you use *depuis combien de temps* in a question, you expect the other person to tell you how long, how much time—how many minutes, how many hours, how many days, weeks, months, years, etc. |

> *Depuis quand habitez-vous cet appartement?* / Since when have you been living in this apartment?
>
> *J'habite cet appartement depuis le premier septembre.* / I have been living in this apartment since September first.

| Tip | Note: When you use *depuis quand* in your question, you expect the other person to tell you since what particular point in time in the past—a particular day, date, month; in other words, since *when*, not *how long*. |

> *Depuis quand êtes-vous malade?* / Since when have you been sick?
>
> *Je suis malade depuis samedi.* / I have been sick since Saturday.
>
> *Depuis quand habitiez-vous l'appartement quand vous avez déménagé?* / Since when had you been living in the apartment when you moved?
>
> *J'habitais l'appartement depuis le cinq avril dernier quand j'ai déménagé.* / I had been living in the apartment since last April fifth when I moved.

Il y a + Length of Time + *que; voici* + Length of Time + *que; voilà* + Length of Time + *que*

● In questions and answers

> *Depuis combien de temps attendez-vous l'autobus?* / How long
> have you been waiting for the bus?
> *J'attends l'autobus depuis vingt minutes.* / I have been waiting for
> the bus for twenty minutes.
> *Voici vingt minutes que je l'attends.* / I have been waiting for it for
> twenty minutes.
> *Voilà vingt minutes que je l'attends.* / I have been waiting for it for
> twenty minutes.
> *Il y a vingt minutes que je l'attends.* / I have been waiting for it for
> twenty minutes.
> *Ça fait vingt minutes que je l'attends.* / I have been waiting for it
> for twenty minutes.

Tip   Note: When you use these expressions, you generally
use them at the beginning of your answer + the verb.
When you use the *depuis* construction, the verb
comes first: *J'attends l'autobus depuis vingt minutes.*

● *Il y a* + length of time

Il y a + length of time means "ago." Do not use *que* in this
construction as in the above examples because the meaning
is entirely different.

> *Madame Martin est partie il y a une heure.* / Mrs. Martin left an
> hour ago.
> *L'autobus est arrivé il y a vingt minutes.* / The bus arrived twenty
> minutes ago.

Il y a and *Il y avait* when not talking about time

● *Il y a* and *Il y avait*

Il y a alone means "there is" or "there are" when you are
merely making a statement.

> *Il y a vingt élèves dans cette classe.* / There are twenty students
> in this class.
> *Il y a une mouche dans la soupe.* / There is a fly in the soup.

Il y avait alone means "there was" or "there were" when you are merely making a statement.

> *Il y avait vingt élèves dans cette classe.* / There were (used to be) twenty students in this class.
> *Il y avait deux mouches dans la soupe.* / There were two flies in the soup.

Voici and *Voilà*

These two expressions are used to point out someone or something.

> *Voici un taxi!* / Here's a taxi!
> *Voilà un taxi là-bas!* / There's a taxi over there!
> *Voici ma carte d'identité et voilà mon passeport.* / Here's my ID card and there's my passport.
> *Voici mon père et voilà ma mère.* / Here's my father and there's my mother.

§12.2 BASIC EXPRESSIONS, BEGINNER AND INTERMEDIATE LEVELS

With *à*

à bicyclette / by bicycle, on a bicycle	*à droite* / at (on, to) the right
à bientôt / so long, see you soon	*à gauche* / at (on, to) the left
à cause de / on account of, because of	*à haute voix* / aloud, out loud, in a loud voice
à cette heure / at this time, at the present moment	*à jamais* / forever
à cheval / on horseback	*à l'école* / at (in, to) school
à côté de / beside, next to	*à l'étranger* / abroad, overseas
à demain / until tomorrow, see you tomorrow	*à l'heure* / on time
	à l'instant / instantly

à l'occasion / on the occasion

à la campagne / at (in, to) the country(side)

à la fin / at last, finally

à la fois / at the same time

à la main / in one's hand, by hand

à la maison / at home

à la mode / fashionable, in style, in fashion

à la radio / on the radio

à la recherche de / in search of

à la télé / on TV

à mon avis / in my opinion

à part / aside

à partir de / beginning with

à peine / hardly, scarcely

à peu près / approximately, about, nearly

à pied / on foot

à plus tard / see you later

à présent / now, at present

à propos / by the way

à propos de / about, with reference to, concerning

à quelle heure? / at what time?

à qui est ce livre? / whose is this book?

à quoi bon? / what's the use?

à son gré / to one's liking

à temps / in time

à tour de rôle / in turn

à tout à l'heure / see you in a little while

à tout prix / at any cost

à travers / across, through

à tue-tête / at the top of one's voice, as loud as possible

à vélo / on a bike

à voix basse / in a low voice, softly

à volonté / at will, willingly

à vrai dire / to tell the truth

à vue d'œil / visibly

With *au*

au bas de / at the bottom of

au besoin / if need be, if necessary

au bout de / at the end of, at the tip of

au contraire / on the contrary

au début / at (in) the beginning

au-dessous de / below, beneath

au-dessus de / above, over

au fond de / at the bottom of

au sommet de / at the top of
au lieu de / instead of
au milieu de / in the middle of
au moins / at least
au pied de / at the foot of
au printemps / in the spring (but *en automne, en hiver, en été*)
au revoir / goodbye

au sous-sol / in the basement
au sujet de / about, concerning
au téléphone / on the telephone
café au lait / coffee with milk
rosbif au jus / roast beef with gravy

With *aux*

aux dépens / at the expense
aux pommes frites / with French fries

rire aux éclats / to roar with laughter
sauter aux yeux / to be evident, self-evident

With *aller*

aller / to feel (health): *Comment allez-vous?*
aller à / to be becoming, fit, suit: *Cette robe lui va bien.* / This dress suits her fine. *Sa barbe ne lui va pas.* / His beard does not look good on him.
aller à la chasse / to go hunting
aller à la pêche / to go fishing

aller à la rencontre de quelqu'un / to go to meet someone
aller à pied / to walk, go on foot
aller au fond des choses / to get to the bottom of things
aller chercher / to go get
allons donc! / nonsense! come on, now!

With *avoir*

avoir . . . ans / to be . . . years old: *Quel âge—avez-vous?* / J'ai dix-sept ans.

avoir à + infinitive / to have to

avoir affaire à quelqu'un / to deal with someone

avoir beau + infinitive / to be useless + infinitive, to do something in vain: *Vous avez beau parler; je ne vous écoute pas.* / You are talking in vain; I am not listening to you.

avoir besoin de / to need, to have need of

avoir bonne mine / to look well

avoir chaud / to be (feel) warm (persons)

avoir congé / to have a day off, a holiday

avoir de la chance / to be lucky

avoir de quoi + infinitive / to have the material, means, enough + infinitive: *As-tu de quoi manger?* / Have you something (enough) to eat?

avoir des nouvelles / to receive news

avoir du savoir-faire / to have tact

avoir du savoir-vivre / to have good manners

avoir envie de + infinitive / to have a desire to

avoir faim / to be (feel) hungry

avoir froid / to be (feel) cold (persons)

avoir hâte / to be in a hurry

avoir honte / to be ashamed, to feel ashamed

avoir l'air + adjective / to seem, to look + adjective: *Vous avez l'air malade.* / You look sick. (The adjective can agree with either *air* or the subject. *Madeleine a l'air contente.* or *Madeleine a l'air content.*)

avoir l'air de + infinitive / to appear + infinitive: *Vous avez l'air d'être malade.* / You appear to be sick.

avoir l'habitude de + infinitive / to be accustomed to, to be in the habit of: *J'ai l'habitude de faire mes devoirs avant le dîner.* / I'm in the habit of doing my homework before dinner.

avoir l'idée de + infinitive / to have a notion + infinitive

avoir l'intention de + infinitive / to intend + infinitive

avoir la bonté de + infinitive / to have the kindness

avoir la langue bien pendue / to have the gift of gab

avoir la parole / to have the floor (to speak)

avoir le cœur gros / to be heartbroken

avoir le temps de + infinitive / to have (the) time + infinitive

avoir lieu / to take place

avoir mal / to feel sick

avoir mal à + (place where it hurts) / to have a pain or ache in . . . : *J'ai mal à la jambe.* / My leg hurts. *J'ai mal au dos.* / My back hurts. *J'ai mal au cou.* / I have a pain in the neck.

avoir mauvaise mine / to look ill, not to look well

avoir peine à + infinitive / to have difficulty in + present participle

avoir peur de / to be afraid of

avoir pitié de / to take pity on

avoir raison / to be right (persons)

avoir soif / to be thirsty

avoir sommeil / to be sleepy

avoir son mot à dire / to have one's way

avoir tort / to be wrong (persons)

avoir une faim de loup / to be starving

With *bas*

au bas de / at the bottom of
en bas / downstairs, below
là-bas / over there
A bas les devoirs! / Down with homework!

parler tout bas / to speak very softly
de haut en bas / from top to bottom

With *bien*

bien des / many: *Roger a bien des amis.* / Roger has many friends. *bien entendu* / of course *dire du bien de* / to speak well of	*être bien aise* / to be very glad, happy *tant bien que mal* / rather badly, so-so *bien sûr* / of course

With *bon*

à quoi bon? / what's the use? *bon gré, mal gré* / willing or not, willy nilly *bon marché* / cheap, at a low price *bon pour quelqu'un* / good for someone	*de bon appétit* / with good appetite, heartily *de bon cœur* / gladly, willingly *savoir bon gré à quelqu'un* / to be thankful, grateful to someone

With *ça*

çà et là / here and there *Ça m'est égal.* / It makes no difference to me. *comme ci, comme ça* / so-so	*Ça va?* / Is everything okay? *C'est comme ça!* / That's how it is! *Pas de ça!* / None of that!

With *cela*

Cela est égal. / It's all the same. It doesn't matter. It makes no difference.

Cela m'est égal. / It doesn't matter to me. It's all the same to me.

Cela n'importe. / That doesn't matter.

Cela ne fait rien. / That makes no difference.

Cela ne sert à rien. / That serves no purpose.

Cela ne vous regarde pas. / That's none of your business.

malgré cela / in spite of that

malgré tout cela / in spite of all that

Qu'est-ce que cela veut dire? / What does that mean?

With *ce, c'est, est-ce*

c'est-à-dire / that is, that is to say

C'est aujourd'hui lundi. / Today is Monday.

C'est dommage. / It's a pity. It's too bad.

C'est entendu. / It's understood. It's agreed. All right. OK.

C'est épatant! / It's wonderful!

C'est trop fort! / That's just too much!

n'est-ce pas? / isn't that so? isn't it?, etc.

Qu'est-ce que c'est? / What is it?

Quel jour est-ce aujourd'hui? / What day is it today? *C'est lundi.* / It's Monday.

Qu'est-ce qui s'est passé? / What happened?

With *d'*

changer d'avis / to change one's opinion, one's mind	*d'avance* / in advance, beforehand
comme d'habitude / as usual	*d'habitude* / ordinarily, usually, generally
d'abord / at first	*d'ici longtemps* / for a long time to come
d'accord / okay, agreed	*d'ordinaire* / ordinarily, usually, generally
d'ailleurs / besides, moreover	*tout d'un coup* / all of a sudden
d'aujourd'hui en huit / a week from today	

With *de*

au sommet de / at the top of	*de l'autre côté de* / on the other side of
autour de / around	*de la part de* / on behalf of, from
changer de train / to change trains: *changer de vêtements* / to change clothes	*de nouveau* / again
combien de / how much, how many	*de parti pris* / on purpose, deliberately
de bon appétit / with good appetite, heartily	*de plus* / furthermore
de bon cœur / gladly, willingly	*de plus en plus* / more and more
de bonne heure / early	*de quelle couleur . . . ?* / what color . . . ?
de cette façon / in this way	*de quoi* + infinitive / something, enough + infinitive: *de quoi écrire* / something to write with; *de quoi manger* / something
de jour en jour / from day to day	

or enough to eat; *de quoi vivre* / something or enough to live on

de rien / you're welcome, don't mention it

de rigueur / required, obligatory

de son mieux / one's best

de suite / one after another, in succession

de temps en temps / from time to time, occasionally

de toutes ses forces / with all one's might, strenuously

du côté de / in the direction of, toward

éclater de rire / to burst out laughing

en face de / opposite

entendre parler de / to hear about

être de retour / to be back

être en train de / to be in the act of, in the process of

être temps de + infinitive / to be time + infinitive

faire semblant de + infinitive / to pretend + infinitive

féliciter quelqu'un de quelque chose / to congratulate someone for something

Il n'y a pas de quoi! / You're welcome!

jamais de la vie! / never in one's life! never! out of the question!

jouer de / to play (a musical instrument)

manquer de + infinitive / to fail to, to almost do something: *Victor a manqué de se noyer.* / Victor almost drowned.

mettre de côté / to lay aside, to save

pas de mal! / no harm!

près de / near

quelque chose de + adjective / something + adjective: *J'ai bu quelque chose de bon!* / I drank something good!

Quoi de neuf? / What's new?

Rien de neuf! / Nothing's new!

tout de même / all the same

tout de suite / immediately, at once

venir de + infinitive / to have just done something; *Je viens de manger.* / I have just eaten.

With *du*

dire du bien de quelqu'un / to speak well of someone	*du matin au soir* / from morning until night
dire du mal de quelqu'un / to speak ill of someone	*du moins* / at least
donner du chagrin à quelqu'un / to give someone grief	*du reste* / besides, in addition, furthermore
du côté de / in the direction of, toward	*montrer du doigt* / to point out, to show, to indicate by pointing
	pas du tout / not at all

With *en*

de jour en jour / from day to day	*en bateau* / by boat
de temps en temps / from time to time	*en bois, en pierre, en* + a material / made of wood, of stone, etc.
en anglais, en français, etc. / in English, in French, etc.	*en chemin de fer* / by train
en arrière / backwards, to the rear, behind	*en dessous (de)* / underneath
en automne, en hiver, en été / in the fall, in winter, in summer (But "in the springtime" is *au printemps*.)	*en dessus (de)* / above, on top, over
	en effet / in fact, indeed, yes, indeed
en automobile / by car	*en face de* / opposite
en avion / by plane	*en famille* / as a family
en avoir plein le dos / to be sick and tired of something	*en haut* / upstairs, above
	en huit jours / in a week
en bas / downstairs, below	*en même temps* / at the same time
	en panne / broken down, out of order

en plein air / in the open air, outdoors

en retard / late, not on time

en tout cas / in any case, at any rate

en toute hâte / with all possible speed, haste

en ville / downtown, in (at, to) town

En voilà assez! / Enough of that!

en voiture / by car: *en voiture!* / all aboard!

être en train de + infinitive / to be in the act of + present participle, to be in the process of, to be busy + present participle

Je vous en prie. / I beg you. You're welcome.

mettre en pièces / to tear to pieces, to break into pieces

voir tout en rose / to see the bright side of things, to be optimistic

With *être*

être à l'heure / to be on time

être à quelqu'un / to belong to someone: *Ce livre est à moi.* / This book belongs to me.

être au courant de / to be informed about

être bien / to be comfortable

être d'accord avec / to agree with

être de retour / to be back

être en retard / to be late, not to be on time

être en train de + infinitive / to be in the act of, to be in the process of, to be busy + present participle

être en vacances / to be on vacation

être enrhumé / to have a cold, be sick with a cold

être pressé(e) / to be in a hurry

Quelle heure est-il? / What time is it? *Il est une heure.* / It is one o'clock. *Il est deux heures.* / It is two o'clock.

With *faire*

Cela ne fait rien. / That doesn't matter.

Comment se fait-il? / How come?

faire à sa tête / to have one's way

faire attention (à) / to pay attention (to)

faire beau / to be pleasant, nice weather

faire bon accueil / to welcome

faire chaud / to be warm (weather)

faire de l'autostop / to hitchhike

faire de son mieux / to do one's best

faire des châteaux en Espagne / to build castles in the air

faire des emplettes; faire des courses; faire du shopping / to do or to go shopping

faire des progrès / to make progress

faire du bien à quelqu'un / to do good for someone

faire du lèche-vitrines / to go window-shopping

faire du vélo / to ride a bike

faire exprès / to do on purpose

faire face à / to oppose, to face, to face up to

faire froid / to be cold (weather)

faire jour / to be daylight

faire la bête / to act like a fool

faire la connaissance de quelqu'un / to make the acquaintance of someone, meet someone for the first time

faire la cuisine / to do the cooking

faire la grasse matinée / to sleep late in the morning

faire la lessive / to do the laundry

faire (une) la malle / to pack (a) the trunk

faire la queue / to line up, to get in line, to stand in line

faire la vaisselle / to do (wash) the dishes

faire le ménage / to do housework

faire les bagages / to pack the baggage, luggage

faire les valises / to pack the suitcases, valises

faire mal à quelqu'un / to hurt, to harm someone

faire nuit / to be night(time)

faire peur à quelqu'un / to frighten someone

faire plaisir à quelqu'un / to please someone

faire sa toilette / to wash and dress oneself

faire ses adieux / to say goodbye

faire son possible / to do one's best

faire suivre le courrier / to forward mail

faire un tour / to go for a stroll

faire un voyage / to take a trip

faire une partie de / to play a game of

faire une promenade / to take a walk

faire une visite / to pay a visit

faire venir quelqu'un / to have someone come: *Il a fait venir le docteur.* / He had the doctor come.

faire venir l'eau à la bouche / to make one's mouth water

Faites comme chez vous! / Make yourself at home!

Que faire? / What is to be done?

Quel temps fait-il? / What's the weather like?

With *mieux*

aimer mieux / to prefer, like better

aller mieux / to feel better (person's health): *Êtes-vous toujours malade?* / Are you still sick? *Je vais mieux, merci.* / I'm feeling better, thank you.

de son mieux / one's best

faire de son mieux / to do one's best

tant mieux / so much the better

valoir mieux / to be better (worth more), to be preferable

With *non*

Je crois que non. / I don't think so.	*Non merci!* / No, thank you!
Mais non! / Of course not!	*J'espère bien que non.* / I hope not.

With *par*

par bonheur / fortunately
par-ci; par-là / here and there
par conséquent / consequently, therefore
par-dessous / under(neath)
par-dessus / over (the top of)
par exemple / for example
par hasard / by chance
par ici / through here, this way, in this direction
par jour / per day, daily
par la fenêtre / out, through the window
par-là / through there, that way, in that direction

par malheur / unfortunately
par mois / per month, monthly
par semaine / per week, weekly
par tous les temps / in all kinds of weather
apprendre par cœur / to learn by heart, memorize
finir par + infinitive / to end up + present participle: *Ils ont fini par se marier.* / They ended up by getting married.
jeter l'argent par la fenêtre / to waste money

With *plus*

de plus / furthermore, besides, in addition
de plus en plus / more and more
n'en pouvoir plus / to be exhausted, not to be able to go on any longer: *Je n'en peux plus!* / I can't

go on any longer!
Plus ça change plus c'est la même chose. / The more it changes, the more it remains the same.
une fois de plus / once more, one more time

With *quel*

Quel âge avez-vous? / How old are you? *Quel garçon!* / What a boy!	*Quel jour est-ce aujourd'hui?* / What day is it today?

With *quelle*

De quelle couleur est (sont) . . . ? / What color is (are) . . . ? *Quelle fille!* / What a girl!	*Quelle heure est-il?* / What time is it? *Quelle chance!* / What luck!

With *quelque chose*

quelque chose à + infinitive / something + infinitive: *J'ai quelque chose à lui dire.* / I have something to say to him (to her).	*quelque chose de* + adjective / something + adjective: *J'ai quelque chose d'intéressant à vous dire.* / I have something interesting to tell you.

With *quoi*

à quoi bon? / what's the use? *avoir de quoi* + infinitive / to have something (enough) + infinitive: *Avez-vous de quoi écrire?* / Do you have something to write with?	*avoir de quoi manger* / to have something to eat *Il n'y a pas de quoi!* / You're welcome! *Quoi de neuf?* / What's new?

With *rien*

Cela ne fait rien. / That doesn't matter.	*de rien* / you're welcome, don't mention it
Cela ne sert à rien. / That serves no purpose.	*Rien de neuf!* / Nothing's new!

With *tant*

tant bien que mal / so-so	*Je t'aime tant!* / I love you so much!
tant mieux / so much the better	*tant de choses* / so many things
tant pis / so much the worse	
J'ai tant de travail! / I have so much work!	

With *tous*

tous (les) deux / both (m. plural)	*tous les matins* / every morning
tous les ans / every year	*tous les soirs* / every evening
tous les jours / every day	*tous les mois* / every month

With *tout*

après tout / after all	*tout d'abord* / first of all
en tout cas / in any case, at any rate	*tout d'un coup* / all of a sudden
pas du tout / not at all	*tout de même!* / all the same! just the same!
tout à coup / suddenly	*tout de suite* / immediately, at once, right away
tout à fait / completely, entirely	*tout le monde* / everybody
tout à l'heure / a little while ago, in a little while	*tout le temps* / all the time

With *toute*

en toute hâte / with all possible speed, in great haste	*toutes (les) deux* / both (f. plural)
toute chose / everything	*toutes les nuits* / every night
de toutes ses forces / with all one's might	

With *y*

il y a + length of time / ago: *il y a un mois* / a month ago	*Il n'y a pas de quoi.* / You're welcome.
il y a / there is, there are	*y compris* / including
il y avait . . . / there was (there were) . . .	*Allez-y!* (polite) or *Vas-y!* (familiar) / Go ahead!

Dates, Days, Months, Seasons

§13.1 Dates

Quelle est la date aujourd'hui? / What's the date today?

C'est aujourd'hui le premier octobre. / Today is October first.
C'est aujourd'hui le deux novembre. / Today is November second.
C'est quel jour aujourd'hui? or *Quel jour sommes-nous aujourd'hui?* / What day is it today?
C'est lundi. / It's Monday.
C'est aujourd'hui mardi. / Today is Tuesday.

Quand êtes-vous né(e)? / When were you born?
Je suis né(e) le vingt-deux août, mil neuf cent soixante-six. / I was born on August 22, 1966.

Use the cardinal numbers for dates, except "the first," which is *le premier.*

§13.2 Days

The days of the week, which are all masculine, are:

dimanche / Sunday	*jeudi* / Thursday
lundi / Monday	*vendredi* / Friday
mardi / Tuesday	*samedi* / Saturday
mercredi / Wednesday	

§13.3 Months

The months of the year, which are all masculine, are:

janvier / January	*juillet* / July
février / February	*août* / August
mars / March	*septembre* / September
avril / April	*octobre* / October
mai / May	*novembre* / November
juin / June	*décembre* / December

To say "in" + the name of the month, use *en: en janvier, en février,* OR *au mois de janvier, au mois de février* / in the month of January, etc.

§13.4 Seasons

The seasons of the year, which are all masculine, are:

le printemps / spring	*l'automne* / fall
l'été / summer	*l'hiver* / winter

 Tip   *En hiver*, you shiver.

To say "in" + the name of the season, use *en* except with *printemps: au printemps, en été, en automne, en hiver* / in spring, in summer, in autumn, in winter.

§14.

Telling Time

§14.1 TIME EXPRESSIONS YOU OUGHT TO KNOW

Quelle heure est-il? / What time is it?

Il est une heure. / It is one o'clock.

Il est une heure dix. / It is ten minutes after one.

Il est une heure et quart. / It is a quarter after one.

Il est deux heures et demie. / It is half past two; it is two thirty.

Il est trois heures moins vingt. / It is twenty minutes to three.

Il est trois heures moins le quart. / It is a quarter to three.

Il est midi. / It is noon.

Il est minuit. / It is midnight.

à quelle heure? / at what time?

à une heure / at one o'clock

à une heure précise / at exactly one o'clock

à deux heures pile / at two o'clock on the dot

à deux heures précises / at exactly two o'clock

à neuf heures du matin / at nine in the morning

à trois heures de l'après-midi / at three in the afternoon

à dix heures du soir / at ten in the evening

à l'heure / on time

à temps / in time

vers trois heures / around three o'clock; about three o'clock

un quart d'heure / a quarter of an hour; a quarter hour

une demi-heure / a half hour

Il est midi et demi / It is twelve thirty; It is half past twelve (noon).

Il est minuit et demi. / It is twelve thirty; It is half past twelve (midnight).

- In telling time, *Il est* + the hour is used, whether it is one or more than one, *e.g., Il est une heure. Il est deux heures*.
- If the time is after the hour, state the hour, then the minutes: *Il est une heure dix*.
- The conjunction *et* is used with *quart* after the hour and with *demi* or *demie: Il est une heure et quart. Il est une heure et demie. Il est midi et demi*.

    The masculine form *demi* is used after a masculine noun: *Il est midi et demi*. The feminine form *demie* is used after a feminine noun: *Il est deux heures et demie*.

    Demi remains *demi* when before a feminine or masculine noun, and is joined to the noun with a hyphen: *une demi-heure*.

- If the time expressed is before the hour, *moins* is used: *Il est trois heures moins vingt*.
- A quarter to the hour is *moins le quart*.
- To express A.M. use *du matin*; to express P.M. use *de l'après-midi* if the time is in the afternoon; *du soir* if in the evening.

§14.2 "OFFICIAL" TIME EXPRESSIONS

Another way to tell time is the official time used by the French government on radio and TV, in railroad and bus stations, and at airports.

- It is the twenty-four-hour system.
- In this system, *quart, demi, demie, moins*, and *et* are not used.
- When you hear or see the stated time, if the number is less than twelve, it is A.M. time, except for *24 heures,* which is midnight; *zéro heure* is also midnight. When the hour is greater than 12 (that is, from 13 through 23), subtract twelve from the number you see or hear.

Examples:

Il est dix heures trente. / It is 10:30 A.M.
Il est treize heures. / It is 1:00 P.M.
Il est quinze heures. / It is 3:00 P.M.
Il est vingt heures trente. / It is 8:30 P.M.
Il est minuit. / It is midnight.
Il est seize heures trente. / It is 4:30 P.M.
Il est dix-huit heures quinze. / It is 6:15 P.M.
Il est vingt heures quarante-cinq. / It is 8:45 P.M.
Il est vingt-deux heures cinquante. / It is 10:50 P.M.

The abbreviation for *heure* or *heures* is *h*.

Examples:

Il est 20 h. 20. / It is 8:20 P.M.
Il est 15 h. 50. / It is 3:50 P.M.
Il est 23 h. 30. / It is 11:30 P.M.

---

§15.

Talking About the Weather

Quel temps fail-il? / What's the weather like?

WITH *Il fait . . .*

Il fait beau. / The weather is fine. The weather is beautiful.
Il fait beau temps. / The weather is beautiful.
Il fait chaud. / It's warm.
Il fait clair. / It is clear.
Il fait doux. / It's mild.
Il fait du soleil. / It's sunny. (You can also say *Il fait soleil.*)
Il fait du tonnerre. / It's thundering. (OR: *Il tonne.*)
Il fait du vent. / It's windy.
Il fait frais. / It is cool.
Il fait froid. / It's cold.
Il fait humide. / It's humid.
Il fait mauvais. / The weather is bad.

WITH *Il fait un temps . . .*

Il fait un temps affreux. / The weather is frightful.
Il fait un temps calme. / The weather is calm.
Il fait un temps couvert. / The weather is cloudy.
Il fait un temps lourd. / It's muggy.
Il fait un temps magnifique. / The weather is magnificent.
Il fait un temps superbe. / The weather is superb.

WITH *Le temps* + VERB . . .

Le temps menace. / The weather is threatening.
Le temps se gâte. / The weather is getting bad.
Le temps se met au beau. / The weather is getting beautiful.
Le temps se met au froid. / It's getting cold.
Le temps se rafraîchit. / The weather is getting cool.

WITH *Le ciel est . . .*

Le ciel est bleu. / The sky is blue.
Le ciel est calme. / The sky is calm.
Le ciel est couvert. / The sky is cloudy.
Le ciel est gris. / The sky is gray.

WITH OTHER VERBS

Il gèle. / It's freezing.
Il grêle. / It's hailing.
Il neige. / It's snowing.
Il pleut. / It's raining.
Il tombe de la grêle. / It's hailing.

§16.

Numbers

Cardinal Numbers: 1 to 1000

0 *zéro*	40 *quarante*
1 *un, une*	41 *quarante et un*
2 *deux*	42 *quarante-deux*, etc.
3 *trois*	
4 *quatre*	50 *cinquante*
5 *cinq*	51 *cinquante et un*
6 *six*	52 *cinquante-deux*, etc.
7 *sept*	
8 *huit*	60 *soixante*
9 *neuf*	61 *soixante et un*
10 *dix*	62 *soixante-deux*, etc.
11 *onze*	
12 *douze*	70 *soixante-dix*
13 *treize*	71 *soixante et onze*
14 *quatorze*	72 *soxiante-douze*, etc.
15 *quinze*	
16 *seize*	80 *quatre-vingts*
17 *dix-sept*	81 *quatre-vingt-un*
18 *dix-huit*	82 *quatre-vingt-deux*, etc.
19 *dix-neuf*	
	90 *quatre-vingt-dix*
20 *vingt*	91 *quatre-vingt-onze*
21 *vingt et un*	92 *quatre-vingt-douze*,
22 *vingt-deux*, etc.	etc.
30 *trente*	100 *cent*
31 *trente et un*	101 *cent un*
32 *trente-deux*, etc.	102 *cent deux*, etc.

200 *deux cents* 201 *deux cent un* 202 *deux cent deux*, etc.	800 *huit cents* 801 *huit cent un* 802 *huit cent deux*, etc.
300 *trois cents* 301 *trois cent un* 302 *trois cent deux*, etc.	900 *neuf cents* 901 *neuf cent un* 902 *neuf cent deux*, etc.
400 *quatre cents* 401 *quatre cent un* 402 *quatre cent deux*, etc.	1000 *mille*
500 *cinq cents* 501 *cinq cent un* 502 *cinq cent deux*, etc.	
600 *six cents* 601 *six cent un* 602 *six cent deux*, etc.	**Tip** If you're not sure that *vingt* is spelled with *ng* or *gn*, note this:
700 *sept cents* 701 *sept cent un* 702 *sept cent deux*, etc.	$$\begin{array}{ccc} V\ I & N & G\ T \\ T\ W\ E & N & T\ Y \end{array}$$

Tip Pronounce *seize* (16) as in English "**Says** who?"

Simple Arithmetical Expressions

deux et deux font quatre	$2 + 2 = 4$
trois fois cinq font quinze	$3 \times 5 = 15$
douze moins dix font deux	$12 - 10 = 2$
dix divisés par deux font cinq	$10 \div 2 = 5$

Fractions

$\frac{1}{2}$	*un demi*	a (one) half
$\frac{1}{3}$	*un tiers*	a (one) third
$\frac{1}{4}$	*un quart*	a (one) fourth
$\frac{1}{5}$	*un cinquième*	a (one) fifth

Approximate Amounts

une dizaine	about ten
une quinzaine	about fifteen
une vingtaine	about twenty
une trentaine	about thirty
une quarantaine	about forty
une cinquantaine	about fifty
une soixantaine	about sixty
une centaine	about a hundred
un millier	about a thousand

Tip You can remember that *une quarantaine* is about 40 because there are 40 days in a "quarantine."

Ordinal Numbers: First to Fiftieth

first	*premier, première*	1st	1er, 1re
second	*deuxième (second, seconde)*	2nd	2^e
third	*troisième*	3rd	3^e
fourth	*quatrième*	4th	4^e
fifth	*cinquième*	5th	5^e

sixth	*sixième*	6th	6^e
seventh	*septième*	7th	7^e
eighth	*huitième*	8th	8^e
ninth	*neuvième*	9th	9^e
tenth	*dixième*	10th	10^e
eleventh	*onzième*	11th	11^e
twelfth	*douzième*	12th	12^e
thirteenth	*treizième*	13th	13^e
fourteenth	*quatorzième*	14th	14^e
fifteenth	*quinzième*	15th	15^e
sixteenth	*seizième*	16th	16^e
seventeenth	*dix-septième*	17th	17^e
eighteenth	*dix-huitième*	18th	18^e
nineteenth	*dix-neuvième*	19th	19^e
twentieth	*vingtième*	20th	20^e
twenty-first	*vingt et unième*	21st	21^e
twenty-second	*vingt-deuxième*	22nd	22^e
twenty-third	*vingt-troisième*	23rd	23^e
twenty-fourth	*vingt-quatrième*	24th	24^e
twenty-fifth	*vingt-cinquième*	25th	25^e
twenty-sixth	*vingt-sixième*	26th	26^e
twenty-seventh	*vingt-septième*	27th	27^e
twenty-eighth	*vingt-huitième*	28th	28^e
twenty-ninth	*vingt-neuvième*	29th	29^e
thirtieth	*trentième*	30th	30^e
fortieth	*quarantième*	40th	40^e
fiftieth	*cinquantième*	50th	50^e

and so on.

Notice that an ordinal number is generally formed by adding the suffix *-ième* to the cardinal number. Before adding the suffix, we must drop the final mute *e* of a cardinal number, if there is one, as in *treize/treizième; trente/trentième*. If you have difficulty forming the ordinal numbers after 50th, you can usually find them in a standard English-French dictionary.

Some observations:

- You must learn the difference between cardinal and ordinal numbers. If you have trouble distinguishing between the two, just remember that we use cardinal numbers most of the time: *un, deux, trois* (one, two, three), and so on.
- Use ordinal numbers to express a certain order: *premier (première*, if the noun following is feminine), *deuxième, troisième* (first, second, third), and so on.
- *Premier* is the masculine singular form and *première* is the feminine singular form. Examples: *le premier homme* / the first man, *la première femme* / the first woman.
- The masculine singular form *second*, or the feminine singular form *seconde*, is used to mean "second" when there are only two. When there are more than two, *deuxième* is used: *le Second Empire*, because there were only two empires in France, but *la Deuxième République*, because there have been more than two republics in France.
- The raised letters in *1er* are the last two letters in the word *premier*; it is equivalent to our "st" in 1st. The raised letters in *1re* are the last two letters in the word *première*, which is the feminine singular form of "first."

The raised letter *e* after an ordinal number (for example, *2e*) stands for the *-ième* ending of a French ordinal number.

- When referring to sovereigns or rulers, the only ordinal number used is *premier*. For all other designations, the cardinal numbers are used. The definite article "the" is used in English but not in French. Examples:

François 1er	*François Premier*	Francis the First
	BUT	
Louis XIV	*Louis Quatorze*	Louis the Fourteenth

Synonyms

Synonyms are words with the same or nearly the same meaning.

aide n.f., *secours* n.m.	aid, help
aimer mieux v., *préférer*	to like better, prefer
aliment n.m., *nourriture* n.f.	food, nourishment
anneau n.m., *bague* n.f.	ring (on finger)
arriver v., *se passer*	to happen, occur
aussitôt que conj., *dès que*	as soon as
auteur n.m., *écrivain* n.m.	author, writer
bâtiment n.m., *édifice,* n.m.	building, edifice
bâtir v., *construire*	to build, construct
beaucoup de adv., *bien des*	many
bref. brève adj., *court, courte*	brief, short
casser v., *rompre, briser*	to break
causer v., *parler*	to chat, talk
centre n.m., *milieu,* n.m.	center, middle
certain (certaine) adj., *sûr, sûre*	certain, sure
cesser v., *arrêter*	to cease, to stop
chagrin n.m., *souci* n.m.	sorrow, trouble, care, concern
chemin n.m., *route* n.f.	road, route
commencer à + infinitive, v., *se mettre à* + infinitive	to commence, begin, start
conseil n.m., *avis* n.m.	counsel, advice, opinion

adj.: adjective; adv.: adverb; conj.: conjunction; f.: feminine; m.: masculine; n.: noun; prep.: preposition; v.: verb

content, (contente) adj., *heureux (heureuse)*	content, happy
de façon que conj., *de manière que*	so that, in such a way
décéder v., *mourir*	to die
dégoût n.m., *répugnance* n.f.	disgust, repugnance
dérober v., *voler*	to rob, steal
désirer v., *vouloir*	to desire, want
disputer v., *contester*	to dispute, argue, contest
docteur n.m., *médecin*, n.m.	doctor, physician
embrasser v., *donner un baiser*	to embrace, hug; to give a kiss
employer v., *se servir de*	to employ, use, make use of
épouvanter v., *effrayer*	to frighten, terrify, scare
erreur n.f., *faute*, n.f.	error, fault, mistake
espèce n.f., *sorte*, n.f.	species, type, kind, sort
essayer de + infinitive, v., *tâcher de* + infinitive	to try, to attempt + infinitive
façon n.f., *manière*, n.f.	way, manner
fameux, (fameuse) adj., *célèbre*	famous, celebrated
fatigué, (fatiguée) adj., *épuisé, (épuisée)*	tired, fatigued, exhausted
favori, (favorite) adj., *préféré (préférée)*	favorite, preferred
fin n.f., *bout* n.m.	end
finir v., *terminer*	to finish, end, terminate
frémir v., *trembler*	to shiver, quiver, tremble
gaspiller v., *dissiper*	to waste, dissipate
gâter v., *abîmer*	to spoil, ruin, damage

glace n.f., *miroir* n.m.	hand mirror, mirror
grossier, grossière adj., *vulgaire*	gross, vulgar, cheap, common
habiter v., *demeurer*	to live (in), dwell, inhabit
haïr v., *détester*	to hate, detest
image n.f., *tableau* n.m.	image, picture
indiquer v., *montrer*	to indicate, show
jadis adv., *autrefois*	formerly, in times gone by
jeu n.m., *divertissement*, n.m.	game, amusement
labourer v., *travailler*	to labor, work
laisser v., *permettre*	to allow, permit
lier v., *attacher*	to tie, attach
lieu n.m., *endroit*, n.m.	place, spot, location
logis n.m. *habitation* n.f.	lodging, dwelling
lutter v., *combattre*	to struggle, fight, combat
maître n.m. *instituteur*, n.m.	master, teacher, instructor
maîtresse n.f. *institutrice*, n.f.	mistress, teacher, instructor
mauvais (mauvaise) adj., *méchant (méchante)*	bad, mean, nasty
mener v., *conduire*	to lead; to take (someone)
mince adj., *grêle*	thin, slender, skinny
naïf (naïve) adj., *ingénu (ingénue)*	naive, simple, innocent
net (nette) adj., *propre*	neat, clean
noces n.f., *mariage* n.m.	wedding, marriage
œuvre n.f., *travail* n.m.	work
ombre n.f., *obscurité* n.f.	shade, shadow, darkness
ombrelle n.f., *parasol* n.m.	sunshade, parasol, beach umbrella
parce que conj., *car*	because, for
pareil (pareille) adj., *égal (égale)*	similar, equivalent, equal

parvenir à v., *réussir à*	to succeed, to attain
pays n.m., *nation* n.f.	country, nation
pensée n.f., *idée*, n.f.	thought, idea
penser v., *réfléchir*	to think, reflect
penser à v., *songer à*	to think of; to dream of
professeur n.m., *maître*, n.m., *maîtresse*, n.f.	professor, teacher
puis adv., *ensuite*	then, afterwards
quand conj., *lorsque*	when
quelquefois adv., *parfois*	sometimes, at times
se rappeler v., *se souvenir de*	to recall, to remember
rester v., *demeurer*	to stay, to remain
sérieux (sérieuse) adj., *grave*	serious, grave
seulement adv., *ne* + verb + *que*	only
soin n.m., *attention* n.f.	care, attention
soulier n.m., *chaussure* n.f.	shoe, footwear
tout de suite adv., *immédiatement*	right away, immediately
triste adj., *malheureux (malheureuse)*	sad, unhappy
vêtements n.m., *habits*, n.m.	clothes, clothing
visage n.m, *figure* n.f.	face
vite adv., *rapidement*	quickly, rapidly

Tip   *Bref* (*brève,* f.) is brief and *court* (*courte,* f.) is short because it contains the English word "curt" (brief, short).

Tip   *Une chaussure* is a shoe because it contains *sur* / on, and you put it on your foot.

Tip   *Une chaussette* is a sock because it's something like an anklet(te) sock.

| Tip |

Une parole is a spoken word because when a prisoner is on "*parole*" he gives his word that he will behave in a civil manner.

| Tip |

When you give someone *conseil*, you give him counsel, advice.

| Tip |

When you *embrasser* a person, you put your *bras* / arms around that person.

§18.

Antonyms

Antonyms are words with opposite meanings.

absent (absente) adj, absent	*présent (présente)* adj., present
acheter v., to buy	*vendre* v., to sell
agréable adj., pleasant, agreeable	*désagréable* adj., unpleasant, disagreeable
aimable adj., kind	*méchant (méchante)* adj., mean, nasty
aller v., to go	*venir* v., to come
ami (amie) n., friend	*ennemi (ennemie)* n., enemy
s'amuser refl. v., to enjoy oneself, to have a good time	*s'ennuyer* refl. v., to be bored
ancien (ancienne) adj., old, ancient	*nouveau (nouvel, nouvelle)* adj., new
avant prep., before	*après* prep., after
bas (basse) adj., low	*haut (haute)* adj., high
beau (bel, belle) adj., beautiful, handsome	*laid (laide)* adj., ugly
beaucoup (de) adv., much, many	*peu (de)* adv., little, some
beauté n.f., beauty	*laideur* n.f., ugliness
bête adj., stupid	*intelligent (intelligente)* adj., intelligent
bon (bonne) adj., good	*mauvais (mauvaise)* adj., bad
bonheur n.m., happiness	*malheur* n.m., unhappiness

adj.: adjective; adv.: adverb; conj.: conjunction; f.: feminine; m.: masculine; n.: noun; prep.: preposition v.: verb *chaud (chaude)* adj., hot, warm

froid (froide) adj., cold

cher (chère) adj., expensive

bon marché cheap

content (contente) adj., glad, pleased

mécontent (mécontente) adj., displeased

court (courte) adj., short

long (longue) adj., long

debout adv., standing

assis (assise) adj., seated, sitting

dedans adv., inside

dehors adv., outside

demander v., to ask

répondre v., to reply

dernier (dernière) adj., last

premier (première) adj., first

derrière adv., prep., behind, in back of

devant adv., prep., in front of

dessous adv., prep., below, underneath

dessus adv., prep., above, over

différent (différente) adj., different

pareil (pareille) adj., same, similar

diffcile adj., difficult

facile adj., easy

domestique adj., domestic

sauvage adj., wild

donner v., to give

recevoir v., to receive

droite n.f., right

gauche n.f., left

emprunter v., to borrow

prêter v., to lend

entrer (dans) v., to enter (in, into)

sortir (de) v., to go out (of, from)

est n.m., east

ouest n.m., west

étroit (étroite) adj., narrow

large adj., wide

faible adj., weak

fort (forte) adj., strong

fermer v., to close

ouvrir v., to open

fin n.f., end

commencement n.m. beginning

finir v., to finish

commencer v., to begin; *se mettre à* v., to begin + inf.

gagner v., to win

gai (gaie) adj., gay, happy

grand (grande) adj., large, tall, big

gros (grosse) adj., fat

grossier (grossière) adj., coarse, impolite

heureux (heureuse) adj., happy

ici adv., here

inutile adj., useless

jamais adv., never

jeune adj., young

jeunesse n.f., youth

joli (jolie) adj., pretty

jour n.m., day

léger (légère) adj., light

lentement adv., slowly

mal adv., badly

moderne adj., modern

moins adv., less

monter v., to go up

mourir v., to die

né (née) adj., past part, born

nord n.m., north

nouveau (nouvel, nouvelle) adj., new

obéir (à) v., to obey

ôter v., to remove, to take off

perdre v., to lose

triste adj., sad

petit (petite) adj., small, little

maigre adj., thin

poli (polie) adj., polite

malheureux (malheureuse) adj., unhappy

là-bas adv., there

utile adj., useful

toujours adv., always

vieux (vieil, vieille) adj., old

vieillesse n.f., old age

laid (laide) adj., ugly

nuit n.f., night

lourd (lourde) adj., heavy

vite adv., quickly

bien adv., well

ancien (ancienne) adj., ancient, old

plus adv., more

descendre v., to go down

naître v., to be born

mort (morte) adj., past part. died, dead

sud n.m., south

vieux (vieil, vieille) adj., old

désobéir (à) v., to disobey

mettre v., to put, to put on

oui adv., yes	*non* adv., no
paix n.f., peace	*guerre* n.f., war
paraître v., to appear	*disparaître* v., to disappear
paresseux (paresseuse) adj., lazy	*travailleur (travailleuse)* adj. diligent
partir v., to leave	*arriver* v., to arrive
pauvre adj., poor	*riche* adj., rich
perdre v., to lose	*trouver* v., to find
plancher n.m., floor	*plafond* n.m., ceiling
plein (pleine) adj., full	*vide* adj., empty
poli (polie) adj., polite	*impoli (impolie)* adj., impolite
possible adj., possible	*impossible* adj., impossible
prendre v., to take	*donner* v. to give
près (de) adv., prep., near	*loin (de)* adv., prep., far (from)
propre adj., clean	*sale* adj., dirty
quelque chose pron., something	*rien* pron., nothing
quelqu'un pron., someone, somebody	*personne* pron., nobody, no one
question n.f., question	*réponse* n.f., answer, reply, response
refuser v., to refuse	*accepter* v., to accept
réussir (à) v., to succeed (at, in)	*échouer (à)* v., to fail (at, in)
rire v., to laugh	*pleurer* v., to cry, to weep
sans prep., without	*avec* prep., with
silence n.m., silence	*bruit* n.m., noise
souvent adv., often	*rarement* adv., rarely
sur prep., on	*sous* prep., under
sûr (sûre) adj., sure, certain	*incertain (incertaine)* adj., unsure, uncertain
tôt adv., early	*tard* adv., late
travailler v., to work	*jouer* v., to play

travailleur (travailleuse) adj., diligent, hardworking	*paresseux (paresseuse)* adj., lazy
vie n.f., life	*mort* n.f., death
vivre v., to live	*mourir* v., to die
vrai (vraie) adj., true	*faux (fausse)* adj., false

Tip The verb *mourir* (to die) has one *r* because a person dies once; *nourrir* (to nourish) has two *r*'s because a person is nourished more than once.

Tip The word *dessous* (below, underneath) contains *sous* (under).

Tip The word *dessus* (above, over) contains *sus*, which reminds you of *sur* (on).

Tip *Perdre* means "to lose" because perdition is a place for lost souls.

Tip Detroit, a city in Michigan, is on the Detroit River, which is narrow (*étroit*) in spots.

Tip A floor (*le plancher*) was originally made of wooden planks.

Tip Pronounce *bonne* as in the English word "bun."

Tip You "mount" a mountain when you *monter une montagne*.

| Tip |

You go **a**way when you *pa rtir* and you go **o**ut when you *so rtir*. *Partir* and "away" contain **a**'s. *Sortir* and "go out" contain **o**'s.

| Tip |

If you don't know your right from your left, *droite* contains "it" and so does "right."

§19.

Cognates

In addition to studying synonyms in §17. and antonyms in §18., another good way to increase your vocabulary is to become aware of cognates. A *cognate* is a word whose origin is the same as another word in another language. There are many cognates in French and English whose spelling is sometimes identical or very similar. Most of the time, the meaning is the same or similar; sometimes they appear to be related because of similar spelling, but are not true cognates. You will find a list of these "false cognates" or "tricky words" in §20.

Generally speaking, certain endings, or suffixes, of French words have English equivalents.

Examples:

French Suffix	Equivalent English Suffix	French Word	English Word
-able	-able	*adorable* *aimable*	adorable amiable (likeable)
-aire	-ary	*le dictionnaire*	dictionary
-eux *-euse*	-ous	*fameux* *fameuse*	famous
-ieux *-ieuse*	-ous	*gracieux* *gracieuse*	gracious
-iste	-ist	*le (la) dentiste*	dentist
-ité	-ity	*la qualité*	quality
-ment	-ly	*correctement*	correctly
-mettre	-mit	*admettre*	admit
-oire	-ory	*la mémoire*	memory
-phie	-phy	*la photographie*	photography
-scrire	-scribe	*transcrire*	transcribe

A French word that contains the circumflex accent (^) over a vowel means that there used to be an *s* right after that vowel.

Examples:

hâte / haste	*hôtel* / hostel
pâte / paste	*honnête* / honest
bâtard / bastard	*plâtre* / plaster
bête / beast	*île* / isle
fête / feast	*vêpres* / vespers
mât / mast	*prêtre* / priest
château / castle	

But you don't always get a cognate if you insert an *s* right after the vowel that contains a circumflex.

Examples:

gâteau / cake	*bêler* / to bleat
bâtiment / building	*âme* / soul

Tip	If you confuse *le gâteau* (cake) with *le bateau* (boat) because you can't remember which one contains the circumflex accent, remember that the ^ in gâteau is the icing on top of the cake!

§20.

Tricky Words

"False friends" (**"faux amis"**/*foh-zamee*) are look-alikes but have different meanings.

There are French words that look like English words but they do not have the same or even similar meaning at all. You must know the following French words and their real meanings. How many others can you think of? Share them with your friends who are studying French. It's a fun way to help build your French vocabulary.

actualités n.f., pl. news reports

actuel adj. present, present-day

actuellement adv. at present

addition n.f. bill (check)

assister v. to attend

attendre v. to wait (for)

belle adj., fem. beautiful

bénir v. to bless

bibliothèque n.f. library (Say *une bibliothèque* when you mean "a library" and *une librairie* when you want to say "a bookstore.")

blesser v. to wound (*Blesser* does not mean "to bless." See *bénir* above.)

cabinet n.m. office; study

car conj. because

causer v. to chat; to cause

cave n.f. cellar, basement

chair n.f. flesh

chargé adj. burdened, loaded

chat n.m. cat

chose n.f. thing

coin n.m. corner

comment adv. how

conférence n.f. lecture

crâne n.m. skull

crayon n.m. pencil

crier v. to shout, cry out

dent n.f. tooth

éditeur n.m. publisher

essence n.f. gasoline

éventuel, éventuelle adj. possible

éventuellement adv. possibly

fin n.f. end
flèche n.f. arrow
fort adj., n. strong
front n.m. forehead

grand adj., m. tall, big, large
grave adj. serious

haïr v. to hate

ignorer v. to be unaware of

journal n.m. newspaper
journée n.f. all day long

large adj. wide, broad
lecture n.f. reading
librairie n.f. bookstore (Say *une librairie* when you want to say "a bookstore" and *une bibliothèque* when you mean "a library.")

magasin n.m. store
main n.f. hand
marine n.f. navy; seascape
médecin n.m. doctor, physician
médecine n.f. medicine (study of)
médicament n.m. medicine
mine n.f. facial appearance
monnaie n.f. change (coins)

occasion n.f. opportunity

pain n.m. bread
par prep. by
personnel adj. personal
pie n.f. magpie (bird)

pile n.f. battery; pile, heap
place n.f. plaza, place
plate adj., fem. flat
pour prep. for
prune n.f. plum
pruneau n.m. prune

quitter v. to leave

raisin n.m. grape
raisin sec n.m. raisin
râpe n.f. grater (cheese)
regarder v. to look (at)
rester v. to remain
roman n.m. novel
rose adj. pink
rose n.f. rose
rue n.f. street

sable n.m. sand
sac n.m. bag, purse
sale adj. dirty, soiled
sensible adj. sensitive
stage n.m. training course of study
stylo n.m. pen

travail n.m. work; *travailler* v. to work (In English, a travail is very difficult or painful work. If you want to say "to travel," the correct translation is *voyager*.)

user v. to wear out

vent n.m. wind (air)
vie n.f. life
voyager v. to travel

§21.

How to Ask a Question

- To ask a question, put **est-ce que** in front of the subject.

    Est-ce que vous parlez français? Do you speak French?
    À quelle heure **est-ce que** le At what time does the
    train part? train leave?

- If the first letter of the subject is a vowel or silent *h*, drop **e** in **que** and add an apostrophe.

    Est-ce qu'il joue? Is he playing?
    Est-ce qu'Hélène est jolie? Is Helen pretty?

- If your question is in the negative, put **ne** in front of the verb and **pas** after it.

    Est-ce que tu **ne** travailles **pas**? Aren't you working?
    Est-ce que vous **n'**avez **pas** Don't you have
    d'argent? any money?

- Instead of using **est-ce que**, you may use the inverted form. Move the subject pronoun and put it after the verb, joining it with a hyphen.

    Parlez-vous français? Do you speak French?
    Ne parlez-vous **pas** anglais? Don't you speak
    English?

- If the subject pronoun is **je**, do not use the inverted form. Use **est-ce que**. The inverted form with **je** is used only with certain verbs, for example:

    Que sais-je? What do I know?
    Où suis-je? Where am I?
    Ai-je assez d'argent? Do I have enough
    money?

- In the inverted form, if the last letter of the verb is a vowel in the third person singular, insert **-t-** between the verb and the subject pronouns **il**, **elle**, or **on**.

Danse-**t**-il?   Does he dance?
                                    Is he dancing?

À quelle heure arrive-**t**-elle?   At what time is she
                                    arriving?

Où va-**t**-on?   Where is one going?

- In the inverted form, if the subject is a noun, mention the noun first and use the pronoun of the noun.

Le docteur va-**t**-il venir bientôt?   Is the doctor going to
                                         come soon?

§22.

Definitions of Basic Grammatical Terms with Examples in French and English Beginner, Intermediate, and Advanced Levels

Active voice

When we speak or write in the active voice, the subject of the verb performs the action. The action falls on the direct object.

Example:
Everyone loves Janine. / *Tout le monde aime Janine.*
The subject is **everyone** / *tout le monde*. The verb is **loves** / *aime*. The direct object is **Janine**.

See also **passive voice** in this section and in §7.9.

Adjective

An adjective is a word that modifies a noun or a pronoun. In grammar, to modify a word means to describe, limit, expand, or make the meaning particular. In French, an adjective agrees in gender (masculine or feminine) and in number (singular or plural) with the noun or pronoun it modifies.

Examples:
This garden is beautiful. / *Ce jardin est beau.*
She is beautiful. / *Elle est belle.*
The adjective **beautiful** / *beau* modifies the noun **garden** / *jardin*. It is masculine singular because *le jardin* is masculine singular.

The adjective **beautiful** / *belle* modifies the pronoun **She** / *Elle*. It is feminine singular because **she** is feminine singular.

When an adjective modifies a noun (or people) of mixed gender, the masculine plural is used, even if there is only one masculine noun or person:

Marie, Suzanne et Sandra sont *grandes*. / Mary, Suzanne, and Sandra are tall. (Fem. pl.)

Robert, Marie, Suzanne et Sandra sont *grands*. / Robert, Mary, Suzanne, and Sandra are tall. (Masc. pl.)

Review *être* in the verb tables in §7.19. In French, there are different kinds of adjectives. See also **comparative adjective, demonstrative adjective, descriptive adjective, interrogative adjective, limiting adjective, possessive adjective,** and **superlative adjective** in this section.

Adverb

An adverb is a word that modifies a verb, an adjective, or another adverb. An adverb says something about how, when, where, to what extent, or in what way.

Examples:

Jane runs swiftly. / *Jeanne court rapidement*. The adverb **swiftly** / *rapidement* modifies the verb **runs** / *court*. The adverb shows *how* she runs.

Jack is a very good friend. / *Jacques est un très bon ami*. The adverb **very** / *très* modifies the adjective **good** / *bon*. The adverb shows *how good* a friend he is.

The boy is eating too fast now. / *Le garçon mange trop vite maintenant*. The adverb **too** / *trop* modifies the adverb **fast** / *vite*. The adverb shows to what extent he is eating fast. The adverb **now** / *maintenant* tells us when.

The post office is there. / *Le bureau de poste est là*. The adverb **there** / *là* modifies the verb **is** / *est*. It tells us where the post office is.

Mary writes carefully. / *Marie écrit soigneusement*. The adverb **carefully** / *soigneusement* modifies the verb **writes** / *écrit*. It tells us in what way she writes.

Affirmative statement, negative statement

A statement in the affirmative is the opposite of a statement in the negative. To negate an affirmative statement is to make it negative.

Examples:
In the affirmative: I like chocolate ice cream. / *J'aime la glace au chocolat.*

In the negative: I do not like chocolate ice cream. / *Je n'aime pas la glace au chocolat.*

Agreement of adjective with noun

An adjective agrees in both gender (masculine or feminine) and number (singular or plural) with the noun that it modifies.

Examples:
a white house / *une maison blanche.* The adjective *blanche* is feminine singular because the noun *une maison* is feminine singular.

two white houses / *deux maisons blanches.* The adjective *blanches* is feminine plural because the noun *maisons* is feminine plural.

When the nouns are of mixed gender (masculine or feminine), a masculine plural adjective is used, even if only one of the nouns is masculine in gender:

Il portait une chemise et un pantalon *bleus.* / He was wearing a blue shirt and blue pants.

Agreement of past participle of a reflexive verb with its reflexive pronoun

When a reflexive pronoun is the **direct object** of a reflexive verb, the past participle agrees with it in both gender (masculine or feminine) and number (singular or plural). The agreement is determined by looking at the subject to see its gender and number, which is the same as its reflexive pronoun. If the reflexive pronoun is the **indirect object**, an agreement is not made.

Examples:

to wash oneself / *se laver*

She washed herself. / *Elle s'est lavée.* There is a feminine
agreement on the past participle *lavée* (added *e*) with the
reflexive pronoun *se* (here, *s'*) because it serves as a direct
object pronoun. What or whom did she wash? Herself, which
is expressed in *se* (*s'*).

But:

She washed her hair. / *Elle s'est lavé les cheveux.* There is no
feminine agreement on the past participle *lavé* here because
the reflexive pronoun (*se*, here, *s'*) serves as an **indirect object**.
The direct object is *les cheveux*, and it is stated after the verb.
What did she wash? She washed her hair **on herself** (*s'*).

See **reflexive verbs** in the Index. See also **reflexive pronoun**
and **reflexive verb** in this section.

Agreement of past participle with its preceding direct object

When a verb is conjugated with *avoir* in the compound tenses,
agreement is made on the past participle with the direct
object in both gender (masculine or feminine) and number
(singular or plural). Agreement is made when the direct object,
if there is one, *precedes* the verb.

Examples:

Where are the cookies? Paul ate them. / *Où sont les biscuits?*
Paul les a mangés. The verb *a mangés* is in the *passé*
composé; *a manger* is conjugated with *avoir*. There is a plural
agreement on the past participle *mangés* (added *s*) because
the preceding direct object **them** / *les* is masculine plural,
referring to *les biscuits*, which is masculine plural.

Who wrote the letters? Robert wrote them. / *Qui a écrit les*
lettres? *Robert les a écrites.* The verb *a écrites* is in the passé
composé; *écrire* is conjugated with *avoir*. There is a feminine
plural agreement on the past participle *écrites* (added *e* and *s*)
because the preceding direct object **them** / *les* is feminine
plural, referring to *les lettres*, which is feminine plural. A past

participle functions as an adjective. An agreement in gender
and number is not made with an indirect object: Robert talked
to them. / *Robert leur a parlé. Leur* is an indirect object (to them).

Review the *passé composé*. See also **direct object noun** and
direct object pronoun in this list.

Agreement of past participle with the subject

When a verb is conjugated with *être* in the compound tenses,
agreement is made on the past participle with the subject in
both gender (masculine or feminine) and number (singular or
plural).

> **Examples:**
>
> She went to Montreal. / *Elle est allée à Montréal.* The verb *est
> allée* is in the *passé composé; aller* is conjugated with *être.*
> There is a feminine agreement on the past participle *allée*
> (added *e*) because the subject *elle* is feminine singular.
> The boys have arrived. / *Les garçons sont arrivés.* The verb *sont
> arrivés* is in the *passé composé; arriver* is conjugated with *être.*
> There is a plural agreement on the past participle *arrivés*
> (added *s*) because the subject *les garçons* is masculine plural.
> Review verbs conjugated with *avoir* or *être* to form the *passé
> composé* tense in §7.3–1. See also **past participle** and
> **subject** in this section.

Agreement of verb with its subject

A verb agrees in person (1st, 2nd, or 3rd) and in number
(singular or plural) with its subject.

> **Examples:**
>
> Does he always tell the truth? / *Dit-il toujours la vérité?* The verb
> *dit* (of *dire*) is third person singular because the subject *il* / **he**
> is third person singular.
> Where are they going? / *Où vont-ils?* The verb *vont* (of *aller*) is
> third person plural because the subject *ils* / **they** is third person
> plural. Review *aller* in the verb tables in §7.19. For subject
> pronouns in the singular and plural, see §6.1–1.

Antecedent

An antecedent is a word to which a relative pronoun refers.
It comes before the pronoun.

> **Examples:**
>> The girl who is laughing over there is my sister. / *La jeune fille qui rit là-bas est ma soeur.* The antecedent is **girl** / *la jeune fille.* The relative pronoun **who** / *qui* refers to the girl.
>>
>> The car that I bought is expensive. / *La voiture que j'ai achetée est chère.* The antecedent is **car** / *la voiture.* The relative pronoun **that** / *que* refers to the car. Note also that the past participle *achetée* is feminine singular because it refers to *la voiture* (fem. sing.), which precedes the verb. See also **relative pronoun** in this section.

Auxiliary verb

An auxiliary verb is a helping verb. In English grammar, it is
to have. In French grammar, it is *avoir* (to have) or *être* (to be).
An auxiliary verb is used to help form the *passé composé*
tense and the other compound tenses.

> **Examples:**
>> I have eaten. (I ate. I did eat.) / *J'ai mangé.*
>> She has left. (She left. She did leave.) / *Elle est partie.*
>> Review verbs conjugated with either *avoir* or *être* as helping verbs to form the *passé composé* in §7.3–1.

Cardinal number

A cardinal number is a number that expresses an amount,
such as one, two, three, and so on.

See also **ordinal number** in this section.

 Tip
Cardinal numbers are used for counting. "How many cardinals did you count on the fence?" "I counted seven cardinals."

Causative *faire*

In English grammar, a causative verb causes something to be done. In French grammar, the idea is the same. The subject of the verb causes the action expressed in the verb to be carried out by someone else.

Example:

Mr. Reisner is having a house built. / *Monsieur Reisner fait construire une maison.*

Review *faire* in the verb tables in §7.19.

Clause

A clause is a group of words that contains a subject and a predicate. A predicate may contain more than one word. A conjugated verb form is revealed in the predicate.

Example:

Mrs. Coty lives in a small apartment. / *Madame Coty demeure dans un petit appartement.*
The subject is **Mrs. Coty** / *Madame Coty.* The predicate is **lives in a small apartment** / *demeure dans un petit appartement.* The verb is **lives** / *demeure.*

See also **dependent clause, independent clause,** and **predicate** in this section.

Comparative adjective

When making a comparison between two persons or things, an adjective is used to express the degree of comparison in the following ways.

Of the same degree of comparison:

Raymond is **as tall as** his father. / *Raymond est **aussi grand que** son père.*

Of a lesser degree of comparison:

Monique is **less intelligent than** her sister. / *Monique est **moins intelligente que** sa soeur.*

Of a higher degree of comparison:

> This apple is **more delicious than** that apple. / *Cette pomme-ci est **plus délicieuse que** cette pomme-là.*

See **comparative adjectives** and **superlative adjectives** in §5.4–5.

Comparative adverb

An adverb is compared in the same way as an adjective is compared. See **comparative adjective** (above).

Of the same degree of comparison:

> Mr. Bernard speaks **as fast as** Mr. Claude. / *Monsieur Bernard parle **aussi vite que** Monsieur Claude.*

Of a lesser degree of comparison:

> Alice studies **less seriously than** her sister. / *Alice étudie **moins sérieusement que** sa soeur.*

Of a higher degree of comparison:

> Albert works **more slowly than** his brother. / *Albert travaille **plus lentement que** son frère.*

Review **comparative adverbs** and **superlative adverbs** in §8.3–3. See also **superlative adverb** in this section.

Complex sentence

A complex sentence contains one independent clause and one or more dependent clauses.

   Examples:

One independent clause and one dependent clause:

> Jack is handsome but his brother isn't. / *Jacques est beau mais son frère ne l'est pas.* The independent clause is **Jack is handsome**. It makes sense when it stands alone because it expresses a complete thought. The dependent clause is **but his brother isn't**. The dependent clause, which is introduced by the conjunction **but**, does not make complete sense when it stands alone because it depends on the thought expressed in the independent clause.

One independent clause and two dependent clauses:

> Mary likes winter because she loves downhill skiing, but she hates the cold. / *Marie aime l'hiver parce qu'elle adore le ski alpin, mais elle déteste le froid.* The independent clause is **Mary likes winter**. It makes sense when it stands alone because it expresses a complete thought. The first dependent clause is because **she loves downhill skiing**. This dependent clause, which is introduced by the conjunction **because**, does not make complete sense when it stands alone because it depends on the thought expressed in the independent clause. The second dependent clause is **but she hates the cold**. That dependent clause, which is introduced by the conjunction **but**, does not make complete sense either when it stands alone because it depends on the thought expressed in the independent clause. See also **dependent clause** and **independent clause** in this section.

Compound sentence

A compound sentence contains two or more independent clauses.

Example:

> Mrs. Dubois went to the supermarket, bought some groceries, and then returned home. / *Madame Dubois est allée au supermarché, elle a acheté des provisions, et puis elle est rentrée chez elle.* This compound sentence contains three independent clauses. They are independent because they make sense when they stand alone. Review the *passé composé* in the Index. See also **clause** and **independent clause** in this section.

Conjugation

The conjugation of a verb is the fixed order of all its forms showing their inflections (changes) in the three persons of the singular and the three persons of the plural in a particular tense.

In French, there are three major types of regular verb conjugations:

>   1st conjugation type: regular verbs that end in *er;* for example, *donner.*
>
>   2nd conjugation type: regular verbs that end in *ir;* for example, *finir.*
>
>   3rd conjugation type: regular verbs that end in *re;* for example, *vendre.*

Conjunction

A conjunction is a word that connects words or groups of words.

Examples:

>   **and** / *et,* **or** / *ou,* **but** / *mais*
>
>   You **and** I are going downtown. / *Toi **et** moi, nous allons en ville.*
>
>   You can stay home **or** you can come with us. / *Tu peux rester à la maison **ou** tu peux venir avec nous.*

Declarative sentence

A declarative sentence makes a statement.

Example:

>   I have finished the work. / *J'ai fini le travail.*

Review the *passé composé* in §7.8–8.

Definite article

The definite article in French has four forms, and they all mean **the**.

They are: *le, la, l', les,* as in:

>   *le livre* / **the book**, *la maison* / **the house**, *l'école* / **the school**, *les enfants* / **the children**

The definite articles are also used as direct object pronouns.

See **direct object pronoun** in this section. See also **definite articles** in §3.1.

Demonstrative adjective

A demonstrative adjective is an adjective that points something or someone out. It is placed in front of a noun.

Examples:

this book / *ce livre;* **this hotel** / *cet hôtel;* **this child** / *cet enfant;* **this house** / *cette maison;* **these flowers** / *ces fleurs*

See **demonstrative adjectives** in §5.4–2.

Demonstrative pronoun

A demonstrative pronoun is a pronoun that points something or someone out. It takes the place of a noun. It agrees in gender and number with the noun it replaces.

Examples:

I have two apples; do you prefer this one or that one? / *J'ai deux pommes; préférez-vous* **celle-ci** *ou* **celle-là**?
Sorry, but I prefer those. / *Je regrette, mais je préfère* **celles-là**.
Do you like the ones that are on the table? / *Aimez-vous* **celles** *qui sont sur la table?*

For demonstrative pronouns that are neuter, see **neuter** in this section.

Dependent clause

A dependent clause is a group of words that contains a subject and a predicate. It does not express a complete thought when it stands alone. It is called dependent because it depends on the independent clause for a complete meaning. Subordinate clause is another term for dependent clause.

Example:

Mary is absent today because she is sick. / *Marie est absente aujourd'hui parce qu'elle est malade*. The independent clause is **Mary is absent today**. The dependent clause is **because she is sick**. Review *être* in the verb tables in §7.19. See also **clause** and **independent clause** in this section.

Descriptive adjective

A descriptive adjective is an adjective that describes a person, place, or thing.

> **Examples:**
>
> **a pretty girl** / *une jolie jeune fille;* **a handsome boy** / *un beau garçon;* **a small house** / *une petite maison;* **a big city** / *une grande ville;* **an expensive car** / *une voiture chère*

Review descriptive adjectives in §5.4–1. See also **adjective** in this section.

Direct object noun

A direct object noun receives the action of the verb **directly**. That is why it is called a **direct object**, as opposed to an indirect object. A direct object noun is normally placed after the verb.

> **Examples:**
>
> I am writing a letter. / *J'écris une lettre.* The subject is **I** / *J' (Je).* The verb is **am writing** / *écris.* The direct object is the noun **letter** / *une lettre.*
>
> I wrote a letter. / *J'ai écrit une lettre.* The subject is **I** / *J' (Je).* The verb is **wrote** / *ai écrit.* The direct object is the noun **letter** / *une lettre.*

See also **direct object pronoun** in this section.

Direct object pronoun

A direct object pronoun receives the action of the verb **directly**. It takes the place of a direct object noun. In French, a pronoun that is a direct object of a verb is ordinarily placed in front of the verb.

> **Example:**
>
> I am reading the letter. / *Je lis la lettre.*
> I am reading it [the letter]. / *Je la lis.*

A direct object pronoun is placed after the verb and joined with a hyphen in the affirmative imperative.

Example:

Write it [the letter] now. / *Écrivez-la maintenant.*

The direct object pronouns are summed up here:

Person	Singular	Plural
1st 2nd	*me (m')* me *te (t')* you (familiar)	*nous* us *vous* you (singular polite or plural)
3rd	*le (l')* him, it (person or thing) *la (l')* her, it (person or thing)	*les* them (persons or things)

See also **imperative** in this section. Consult the **imperative (command)** in §7.8–15 and **word order in a sentence** in §11.

Disjunctive pronoun

In French grammar, a disjunctive pronoun is a pronoun that is stressed; in other words, emphasis is placed on it.

Examples:

I speak well; he does not speak well. / *Moi, je parle bien; lui, il ne parle pas bien.*
Talk to me. / *Parlez-moi.*

A disjunctive pronoun is also an object of a preposition.

Examples:

She is talking with me. / *Elle parle avec moi.*
I always think of you. / *Je pense toujours à toi.*

The disjunctive pronouns are summed up here:

Person	Singular		Plural	
1st	*moi*	me	*nous*	us
2nd	*toi*	you (familiar)	*vous*	you (singular polite or plural)
3rd	*soi*	oneself		
	lui	him, he	*eux*	them, they (m.)
	elle	her, she	*elles*	them, they (f.)

Ending of a verb

In French grammar, the ending of a verb form changes according to the person and number of the subject and the tense of the verb.

Example:

To form the present indicative tense of a regular -*er* verb like parler, drop the -*er* ending of the infinitive and add the following endings: **-e, -es, -e** for the first, second, and third persons of the singular; -**ons, -ez, -ent** for the first, second, and third persons of the plural.
You then get:

> *je parle, tu parles, il (elle, on) parle*
> *nous parlons, vous parlez, ils (elles) parlent*

See also **stem of a verb** in this section.

Feminine

In French grammar, the gender of a noun, pronoun, or adjective is feminine or masculine, not female or male.

Examples:

	Masculine	
noun	**pronoun**	**adjective**
le garçon	*il*	*grand*
the boy	he	tall
le livre	*il*	*petit*
the book	it	small

	Feminine	
noun	**pronoun**	**adjective**
la femme	*elle*	*grande*
the woman	she	tall
la voiture	*elle*	*petite*
the car	it	small

See also **gender** and **neuter** in this section.

Gender

In French and English grammar, gender means masculine or feminine.

> **Examples:**
> Masculine: **the boy** / *le garçon;* **he, it** / *il;* **the book** / *le livre*
> Feminine: **the girl** / *la jeune fille;* **she, it** / *elle;* **the house** / *la maison*

Gerund

In English grammar, a gerund is a word formed from a verb. It ends in **ing**. Actually, it is the present participle of a verb, but it is not used as a verb; it is used as a noun.

Example:

Seeing is believing. / *Voir c'est croire.*

However, in French grammar, the infinitive form of the verb is used, as in the preceding example, when the verb is used as a noun. In French, **seeing is believing** is expressed as **to see is to believe**.

The French gerund is also a word formed from a verb. It ends in **ant**. It is also the present participle of a verb. As a gerund, it is normally preceded by the preposition *en*.

Example:

En partant, il a claqué la porte. / While leaving, he slammed the door.

See also **present participle** in this section.

Imperative

The imperative is a mood, not a tense. It is used to express a command. In French, it is used in the second person of the singular (*tu*), the second person of the plural (*vous*), and the first person of the plural (*nous*).

Examples:

Fais attention! / Be careful!
Fermez la porte, s'il vous plaît. / Close the door, please.
Mangeons! / Let's eat!

Review the **imperative (command)** with examples in §7.8–15. See also **person (1st, 2nd, 3rd)** in this section.

Indefinite article

In English, the indefinite articles are **a** and **an**, as in **a book, an apple.** They are indefinite because they do not refer to any definite or particular noun.

In French there are two indefinite articles in the singular: one in the masculine form (*un*) and one in the feminine form (*une*).

Examples:

Masculine singular: *un livre* / **a book**
Feminine singular: *une pomme* / **an apple**

In French, they both change to *des* in the plural.

Examples:

I have a brother. / *J'ai un frère;* I have brothers. / *J'ai des frères.*
I have a sister. / *J'ai une soeur;* I have sisters. / *J'ai des soeurs.*
I have an apple. / *J'ai une pomme;* I have apples. / *J'ai des pommes.*

See also **definite article** in this section. Consult §3.1.

Indefinite pronoun

An indefinite pronoun is a pronoun that does not refer to any definite or particular noun.

Examples:

something / *quelque chose;* **someone, somebody** / *quelqu'un, quelqu'une;* **one, "they"** / *on* (3rd pers. sing.) as in *On ne sait jamais.* / One never knows; *On dit qu'il va neiger.* / They say it's going to snow; **each one** / *chacun, chacune;* **anything** / *n'importe quoi.*

Independent clause

An independent clause is a group of words that contains a subject and a predicate. It expresses a complete thought when it stands alone.

Example:

The cat is sleeping under the bed. / *Le chat dort sous le lit.*

See also **clause, dependent clause,** and **predicate** in this section.

Indicative mood

The indicative mood is used in sentences that make a statement or ask a question. The indicative mood is used most of the time when we speak or write in English or French.

Examples:

Where are you going? / *Où allez-vous?*
I am going home now. / *Je vais chez moi maintenant.*

Indirect object noun

An indirect object noun receives the action of the verb *indirectly.*

Example:

I am writing a letter to Mary **or** I am writing Mary a letter. / *J'écris une lettre à Marie.*

The subject is **I** / *Je.* The verb is **am writing** / *écris.* The direct object noun is **a letter** / *une lettre.* The indirect object noun is **to Mary** / *à Marie.* An agreement is not made with an indirect object noun.

See also **indirect object pronoun, direct object noun,** and **direct object pronoun** in this section.

Indirect object pronoun

An indirect object pronoun takes the place of an indirect object noun. It receives the action of the verb **indirectly.** In French a pronoun that is the indirect object of a verb is ordinarily placed in front of the verb.

Example:

I am writing a letter to her **or** I am writing her a letter. / *Je lui écris une lettre.* The indirect object pronoun is **(to) her** / *lui.*

An agreement is not made with an indirect object pronoun. An indirect object pronoun is placed after the verb and is joined with a hyphen in the affirmative imperative.

Example:

Write to her now. / *Écris-lui maintenant.*

The indirect object pronouns are summed up below:

Person	Singular		Plural	
1st	*me* (*m'*) to me		*nous*	to us
2nd	*te* (*t'*)	to you (fam.)	*vous*	to you (singular polite or plural)
3rd	*lui*	to him, to her	*leur*	to them

Review the **imperative (command)** in §7.8–15. See also **indirect object noun** in this section.

Infinitive

An infinitive is a verb form. In English, it is normally stated with the preposition **to**, as in **to talk, to finish, to sell**. In French, the infinitive form of a verb consists of three major types: those of the first conjugation that end in *-er,* those of the second conjugation that end in *-ir,* and those of the third conjugation that end in *-re.*

Examples:

parler / **to talk, to speak**; *finir* / **to finish**; *vendre* / **to sell**

Interjection

An interjection is a word that expresses emotion, a feeling of joy or sadness, an exclamation of surprise, and other exclamations consisting of one or two words.

Examples:

Ah! / *Ah!*
Oh! / *Oh!*
Darn it! / *Zut!*
Whew! / *Ouf!*

Interrogative adjective

An interrogative adjective is an adjective used in a question. It agrees in gender and number with the noun it modifies.

Examples:

What book do you want? / *Quel livre désirez-vous?*
What time is it? / *Quelle heure est-il?*

See also §5.4–3.

Interrogative adverb

An interrogative adverb is an adverb that introduces a question. As an adverb, it modifies the verb.

Examples:

How are you? / *Comment allez-vous?*
How much does this book cost? / *Combien coûte ce livre?*
When are you leaving? / *Quand partez-vous?*

See also §8.3–1.

Interrogative pronoun

An interrogative pronoun is a pronoun that asks a question. There are interrogative pronouns that refer to persons and those that refer to things.

Examples:

Who is on the phone? / *Qui est à l'appareil?*
What are you saying? / *Que dites-vous?* or **Qu'est-ce que** *vous dites?*

Interrogative sentence

An interrogative sentence asks a question.

Example:

What are you doing? / *Que faites-vous?* (inversion) or *Qu'est-ce que vous faites?* (with *qu'est-ce que*)

Intransitive verb

An intransitive verb is a verb that does not take a direct object.

Example:

The professor is talking too fast. / *Le professeur parle trop rapidement.*

An intransitive verb takes an indirect object.

Example:

The professor is talking to us. / *Le professeur nous parle.*

See also **indirect object pronoun** and **transitive verb** in this section.

Irregular verb

An irregular verb is a verb that does not follow a fixed pattern in its conjugation in the various verb tenses.

Examples of basic irregular verbs in French:

aller / **to go**
avoir / **to have**
être / **to be**
faire / **to do, to make**

Review irregular verbs in the present indicative tense and the imperative (command). See also **conjugation** and **regular verb** in this section.

Limiting adjective

A limiting adjective is an adjective that limits a quantity.

Example:

three tickets / *trois billets*

Main clause

Main clause is another term for independent clause.

See **independent clause** in this section.

Masculine

In French grammar, the gender of a noun, pronoun, or adjective is masculine or feminine, not male or female. See also **feminine**, **gender**, and **neuter** in this section.

Mood of verbs

Some grammarians use the term **the mode** instead of **the mood** of a verb. Either term means the manner or *way* in which a verb is expressed. In English and French grammar, a verb expresses an action or state of being in the following three moods (modes, *ways*): the indicative mood, the imperative mood, and the subjunctive mood. In French grammar, there is also the infinitive mood when the whole infinitive is used; for example *voir* and *croire*, as in *Voir c'est croire* / Seeing is believing (literally, to see is to believe). Most of the time in English and French, we speak and write in the indicative mood.

See also **indicative mood** in this section.

Negative statement, affirmative statement

See **affirmative statement** and **negative statement** in this section.

Neuter

A word that is neuter is neither masculine nor feminine. Common neuter demonstrative pronouns are *ce (c')* / **it**, *ceci* / **this**, *cela* / **that**, *ça* / **that**. They are invariable, which means they do not change in gender and number. When you use one of these neuter demonstrative pronouns, you should make a masculine agreement. For example, even if you are talking about pizza (*la pizza*), you say *C'est bon!* because of the neuter *ce (c')*.

Examples:

It's not true / *Ce n'est pas vrai;* it is true / *c'est vrai;* this is true / *ceci est vrai;* that is true / *cela est vrai;* what is that? / *qu'est-ce que c'est que ça?*

There is also the neuter pronoun *le*, as in *Je le pense* / I think so.

For demonstrative pronouns that are not neuter, see **demonstrative pronoun** in this section. See also **feminine** and **gender**.

Noun

A noun is a word that names a person, animal, place, thing, condition or state, or quality.

> **Examples:**
>
> > **the man** / *l'homme*, **the woman** / *la femme*, **the horse** / *le cheval*, **the house** / *la maison*, **the book** / *le livre*, **happiness** / *le bonheur*, **excellence** / *l'excellence* (fem.)

In French, the noun *le nom* is the word for **name** (*Quel est votre nom?* / What is your name?) and also for **noun** (*Un adjectif sert à qualifier un nom.* / An adjective is used to qualify a noun.)

Number

In English and French grammar, number means singular or plural.

> **Examples:**
>
> > Masc. sing.: **the boy** / *le garçon;* **the arm** / *le bras;* **the eye** / *l'oeil*
> >
> > Masc. pl.: **the boys** / *les garçons;* **the arms** / *les bras;* **the eyes** / *les yeux*
> >
> > Fem. sing.: **the girl** / *la jeune fille;* **the house** / *la maison;* **the hen** / *la poule*
> >
> > Fem. pl.: **the girls** / *les jeunes filles;* **the houses** / *les maisons;* **the hens** / *les poules*

Ordinal number

An ordinal number expresses position in a series, such as **first, second, third**, and so on. In English and French grammar, we talk about first person, second person, third person singular or plural regarding subjects and verbs. Review the ordinal numbers and consult the Index. See also **cardinal number,** and **person (1st, 2nd, 3rd)** in this section.

Ordinal numbers are used to describe an order in a sequence. "Tom was tired because he'd taken his fiftieth order of the day."

Orthographical changes in verb forms

An orthographical change in a verb form is a change in spelling.

> **Examples:**
>
> The second letter *c* in the verb *commencer* / **to begin** changes to *ç* if the letter after it is *a, o,* or *u,* as in *nous commençons* / **we begin**. The reason for this spelling change is to preserve the sound of *s* as it is pronounced in the infinitive form *commencer*. Ordinarily, when *a, o,* or *u* follow the letter *c,* the *c* is pronounced as in the sound of *k*. The mark under the letter *ç* is called *une cédille* / a cedilla. Some linguists say it is the lower part of the letter *s* and it tells you to pronounce *ç* as an *s* sound. Other linguists say that the letter *ç* was borrowed from the Greek alphabet's *sigma* (ς), which represents the sound of *s*.
>
> The verb *s'appeler* / **to call oneself, to be named** contains a single *l*. When a verb form is stressed on the syllable containing one *l*, it doubles, as in *je m'appelle...* / **I call myself..., my name is...**

Review orthographically changing verbs in §7.17.

Partitive

In French grammar, the partitive denotes a *part* of a whole. In English, we express the partitive by saying **some** or **any** in front of the noun. In French, we use the following partitive forms in front of the noun:

> Masculine singular: *du* or *de l'*
> Feminine singular: *de la* or *de l'*
> Masculine or feminine plural: *des*
>
> (Note : The plural is rare in the partitive because the partitive is not used for countable things: *des pâtes* / **some pasta**; *des épinards* / **some spinach**. When you use *des* with countable

things, you are not using the partitive. You are using the plural indefinite article: *un ami* (a friend) / *des amis* (friends); *une carotte* (a carrot) / *des carottes* (carrots); *un stylo* (a pen) / *des stylos* (pens). See §3.2.)

Examples:

I have some coffee. / *J'ai du café.*
Bring me some water, please. / *Apportez-moi de l'eau, s'il vous plaît.*
Is there any meat? / *Y a-t-il de la viande?*
Do you have any pasta? / *Avez-vous des pâtes?*

In the negative, these partitive forms change to *de* or *d'*:

I don't have any coffee. / *Je n'ai pas de café.*
I don't want any water. / *Je ne veux pas d'eau.*
There isn't any meat. / *Il n'y a pas de viande.*
No, I don't have any pasta. / *Non, je n'ai pas de pâtes.*

Review the partitive in §3.3.

Passé composé

The name of a commonly used past tense is the *passé composé*. It is defined with examples in French and English. Consult §7.8–8.

Passive voice

When we speak or write in the active voice and change to the passive voice, the direct object becomes the subject, the subject becomes the object of a preposition, and the verb becomes **to be** plus the past participle of the active verb. The past participle functions as an adjective.

Example:

Janine is loved by everyone. / *Janine est aimée de tout le monde.* The subject is **Janine**. The verb is **is** / *est*. The object of the preposition **by** / *de* is **everyone** / *tout le monde*. Compare the preceding sentence with the example in the **active voice** in this section.

Past indefinite tense

In French, this tense is the *passé composé*. See ***passé composé*** in this section and review §7.8–8.

Past participle

A past participle is derived from a verb. It is used to form the compound tenses, such as the *passé composé*. Its auxiliary verb in English is **to have**. In French, the auxiliary verb is *avoir /* **to have** or *être /* **to be**. The auxiliary is part of the verb tense.

Examples with *avoir* as the auxiliary verb:

Elle a mangé. / **She has eaten**. (She ate; she did eat.) The subject is *elle /* **she**. The verb is *a mangé /* **has eaten**. The tense of the verb is the *passé composé*. The auxiliary verb is *a /* **has**. The past participle is *mangé /* **eaten**.

Examples with *être* as the auxiliary verb:

Elle est arrivée. / **She has arrived.** (She arrived; she did arrive.) The verb is *est arrivée /* **has arrived**. The tense of the verb is the *passé composé*. The auxiliary verb is *est /* **has**. The past participle is *arrivée /* **arrived**.

Person (1st, 2nd, 3rd)

Verb forms in a particular tense are learned systematically according to person (1st, 2nd, 3rd) and number (singular, plural).
The following example shows the present indicative tense of the verb *aller /* **to go**:

Singular		Plural	
1st person:	*je vais*	1st person:	*nous allons*
2nd person:	*tu vas*	2nd person:	*vous allez*
3rd person:	*il, elle va*	3rd person:	*ils, elles vont*

Personal pronoun

A personal pronoun refers to a person. Review the subject pronouns in §6.1–1. For examples of other types of pronouns, see also **demonstrative pronoun, direct object pronoun, disjunctive pronoun, indefinite pronoun, indirect object pronoun, interrogative pronoun, reflexive pronoun,** and **relative pronoun** in this section.

Plural

Plural means more than one. See also **person (1st, 2nd, 3rd)** and **singular** in this section.

Possessive adjective

A possessive adjective is an adjective that is placed in front of a noun to show possession. In French, their forms change in gender (masculine or feminine) and number (singular or plural) to agree with the noun they modify.

Examples:

my book / *mon livre*
my books / *mes livres*
my car / *ma voiture*
my cars / *mes voitures*

Predicate

The predicate is the part of the sentence that tells us something about the subject. The main word of the predicate is the verb.

Example:

The tourists are waiting for the tour bus. / *Les touristes attendent l'autocar.*
The subject is **the tourists** / *les touristes*. The predicate is **are waiting for the tour bus** / *attendent l'autocar*. The verb is **are waiting** / *attendent*. The direct object is **the tour bus** / *l'autocar*.

Preposition

A preposition is a word that establishes a rapport between words.

Examples (with, in, on, at, between):

with me / *avec* moi
in the drawer / *dans* le tiroir
on the table / *sur* la table
at six o'clock / *à* six heures
between him and her / *entre* lui et elle

Present indicative tense

This is a commonly used tense. It is defined with examples in French and English in §7.8–1.

Present participle

A present participle is derived from a verb form. In French it is regularly formed like this: Take the *nous* form of the present indicative tense of the verb you have in mind, then drop the ending *ons* and add *ant*. In English, a present participle ends in **ing**.

Examples:

Infinitive	Present Indicative *nous* form	Present participle
chanter	*nous chantons*	*chantant*
to sing	we sing	singing
finir	*nous finissons*	*finissant*
to finish	we finish	finishing
vendre	*nous vendons*	*vendant*
to sell	we sell	selling

Pronoun

A pronoun is a word that takes the place of a noun.

Examples:

l'homme / **il**
the man / **he**
la femme / **elle**
the woman / **she**
l'arbre / **il**
the tree / **it**
la voiture / **elle**
the car / **it**

For examples of other kinds of pronouns, see also **demonstrative pronoun, direct object pronoun, disjunctive pronoun, indefinite pronoun, indirect object pronoun, interrogative pronoun, reflexive pronoun,** and **relative pronoun** in this section.

Reflexive pronoun and reflexive verb

In English, a reflexive pronoun is a personal pronoun that contains **-self** or **-selves**. In French and English, a reflexive pronoun is used with a verb that is called reflexive because the action of the verb falls (is reflected back) on the reflexive pronoun. In French, as in English, there is a required set of reflexive pronouns for a reflexive verb.

Examples:

se laver / to wash oneself
Je me lave. / I wash myself.
se blesser / to hurt oneself
Elle s'est blessée. / She hurt herself.

In French, a reflexive verb is conjugated with *être* to form a compound tense. The French term for a reflexive verb is *un verbe pronominal* because a pronoun goes with the verb. See also **agreement of past participle of a reflexive verb with its reflexive pronoun** in this section.

Regular verb

A regular verb is a verb that is conjugated in the various tenses according to a fixed pattern. For examples, review regular -*er*, -*ir*, and -*re* verbs in the present indicative tense. Consult the Index. See also **conjugation** and **irregular verb** in this section.

Relative pronoun

A relative pronoun is a pronoun that refers to its antecedent.

Example:

The woman who won the award is my mother. / *La femme qui a gagné le prix est ma mère.* The antecedent is **woman** / *la femme*. The relative pronoun **who** / *qui* refers to the woman.

See also **antecedent** in this section.

Sentence

A sentence is a group of words that contains a subject and a predicate. The verb is contained in the predicate. A sentence expresses a complete thought.

Example:

The train leaves from the North Station at two o'clock in the afternoon. / *Le train part de la Gare du Nord à deux heures de l'après-midi.* The subject is **train** / *le train*. The predicate is **leaves from the North Station at two o'clock in the afternoon** / *part de la Gare du Nord à deux heures de l'après-midi*. The verb is **leaves** / *part*.

See also **complex sentence, compound sentence,** and **simple sentence** in this section.

Simple sentence

A simple sentence is a sentence that contains one subject and one predicate. The verb is the core of the predicate. The verb is the most important word in a sentence because it tells us what the subject is doing.

Example:

> Mary is eating an apple from her garden. / *Marie mange une pomme de son jardin.* The subject is **Mary** / *Marie.* The predicate is **is eating** / *mange.* The direct object is **an apple** / *une pomme.* **From her garden** / *de son jardin* is an adverbial phrase. It tells you where the apple came from.

See also **complex sentence** and **compound sentence** in this section.

Singular

Singular means one. See also **person (1st, 2nd, 3rd)** and **plural** in this section.

Stem of a verb

The stem of a verb is what is left after we drop the ending of its infinitive form. It is added to the required endings of a regular verb in a particular verb tense.

Examples:

Infinitive	Ending of infinitive	Stem
donner / to give	*er*	*donn*
choisir / to choose	*ir*	*chois*
vendre / to sell	*re*	*vend*

See also **ending of a verb** in this section.

Subject

A subject is the part of a sentence that is related to its verb. The verb says something about the subject.

Examples:

> Mary and Catherine are beautiful. / *Marie et Catherine sont belles.*
> Peter and Paul are handsome. / *Pierre et Paul sont beaux.*

Subjunctive mood

The subjunctive mood of a verb is used in specific cases; for example, it is used after certain verbs expressing a wish, doubt, emotion, fear, joy, uncertainty, an indefinite expression, an indefinite antecedent, certain conjunctions, and others. Review the present subjunctive mood of *avoir* and *être* in §7.19. See also **mood of verbs** in this section.

Subordinate clause

Subordinate clause is another term for dependent clause. See also **dependent clause** in this section.

Superlative adjective

A superlative adjective is an adjective that expresses the highest degree when making a comparison of more than two persons or things.

Examples:

	Adjective	Comparative	Superlative
(masc.)	*bon* / good	*meilleur* / better	*le meilleur* / (the) best
(fem.)	*bonne* / good	*meilleure* / better	*la meilleure* / (the) best
(masc.)	*mauvais* / bad	*plus mauvais* / worse	*le plus mauvais* / (the) worst
(fem.)	*mauvaise* / bad	*plus mauvaise* / worse	*la plus mauvaise* / (the) worst

See also **comparative adjective** in this list.

Superlative adverb

A superlative adverb is an adverb that expresses the highest degree when making a comparison of more than two persons or things.

Example:

Adverb	Comparative	Superlative
vite / quickly	*plus vite* / more quickly	*le plus vite* / most quickly
	moins vite / less quickly	*le moins vite* / least quickly

Tense of verb

In English and French grammar, tense means time. The tense of the verb indicates the time of the action or state of being. The three major segments of time are past, present, and future. Review the verb tables in §7.19.

Transitive verb

A transitive verb is a verb that takes a direct object.

Example:

I am closing the window. / *Je ferme la fenêtre.* The subject is **I** / *Je.* The verb is **am closing** / *ferme.* The direct object is **the window** / *la fenêtre.* The action of the verb is carried out on the direct object.

See also **intransitive** in this section.

Verb

A verb is a word that expresses action or a state of being.

Example of action:

Nous sommes allées au cinéma hier soir. / We went to the movies last night.
The verb is *sommes allés* / **went**.

Example of state of being:

La jeune fille est heureuse. / The girl is happy.
The verb is *est* / **is**.

Review *aller* and *être* in §7.19.

French-English Vocabulary

à *prep.* at, to

à moins que *conj.* unless

actif, active *adj.* active

aéroport *n.m.* airport

affreusement *adv.* frightfully

ai *v. form of* **avoir**

aimable *adj.* amiable, likeable, pleasant, kind

aimer *v.* to love; **aimer bien** to like

Allemagne *n.f.* Germany

allemand *n.m.* German (language); **Allemand, Allemande** *n.* German (person)

aller *v.* to go; **s'en aller** to go away

allez-vous-en! go away!

allons! let's go!

amèrement *adv.* bitterly

ami, amie *n.* friend

amour *n.m.* love

amusant, amusante *adj.* funny, amusing

an *n.m.* year

ancien, ancienne *adj.* old, ancient

anglais *n.m.* English (language); **Anglais, Anglaise** *n.* English (person)

Angleterre *n.f.* England

appeler *v.* to call; **s'appeler** *reflexive v.* to call oneself, to be named

après *prep., adv.* after; **après-midi** *n.m.* afternoon

arbre *n.m.* tree

argent *n.m.* money

Asie *n.f.* Asia

asseoir *v.* to seat; **s'asseoir** *reflexive v.* to sit down; **asseyez-vous!** sit down!

assez (de) *adv.* enough (of); **assez bien** quite well, well enough

assieds-toi! sit down!

adj.: adjective; adv.: adverb; conj.: conjunction; f.: feminine;
m.: masculine; n.: noun; pl.: plural; prep.: preposition;
pron.: pronoun; sing.: singular; v.: verb

au to the, at the; contraction of **à** + **le**

aujourd'hui *adv.* today

aussi *adv.* also, too

aussi . . . que *conj.* as . . . as

Australie *n.f.* Australia

auteur *n.m.,* **auteure** *n.f.* author

autre *adj.* other; *pron.* another

autrefois *adv.* formerly

aux to the, at the; contraction of **à** + **les**

avec *prep.* with

avez *v. form of* **avoir**

avocat *n.m.* lawyer; **une avocate** woman lawyer

avoir *v.* to have

bas *n.m.* stocking; *adv.* low; **en bas** down, downstairs; *adj.* **bas, basse** low

beau *adj. m.* handsome, beautiful

beaucoup (de) *adv.* many, much (of)

bel *adj. m.* handsome, beautiful (Use *bel* before a vowel or mute *h:* un *bel hôtel* / a beautiful hotel)

belle *adj. f.* beautiful, handsome

bénir *v.* to bless

besoin *n.m.* need; **avoir besoin de** to need, to have need of

bibliothèque *n.f.* library

bien *adv.* well

bientôt *adv.* soon

billet *n.m.* ticket, note

blanc, blanche *adj.* white

blesser *v.* to injure, to wound

boire *v.* to drink

bon, bonne *adj.* good

bonbons *n.m.* candies

bouche *n.f.* mouth (of a person); **la gueule** (mouth of an animal)

but *n.m.* goal

ça *pron.* shortening of **cela**

cadeau *n.m.* gift, present

café *n.m.* coffee

cahier *n.m.* notebook

campagne *n.f.* country(side)

catholique *n.m.f.* Catholic

ce *demons. adj.* this; **ce stylo** this pen; **ce livre** this book; **ce garçon** this boy

cela *pron.* that; **Aimez-vous cela?** Do you like that?

chanter *v.* to sing

chanteur, chanteuse *n.m.f.* singer

chapeau *n.m.* hat

chaque *adj.* each

chaud, chaude *adj.* warm, hot

chaussette *n.f.* sock

chaussure *n.f.* shoe

chef *n.m.* chief, boss, chef

cheveu, cheveux *n.m.* hair

chez *prep.* at the place of, at the home of, at the shop of; **chez moi** at my place

choisir *v.* to choose, to select

chose *n.f.* thing; **quelque chose** something

cinéma *n.m.* movies (theater)

clé, clef *n.f.* key

coin *n.m.* corner

combien (de) *adv.* how much (of), how many (of)

comprendre *v.* to understand

copain *n.m.*, **copine** *n.f.* pal, buddy

cravate *n.f.* necktie

crayon *n.m.* pencil

croire *v.* to believe

cruel, cruelle *adj.* cruel

dame *n.f.* lady

dans *prep.* in

de *prep.* of, from

dehors *adv.* outside

déjà *adv.* already; **déjà vu** already seen

dent *n.f.* tooth

depuis *adv.* since; **depuis longtemps** for a long time

dernier, dernière *adj.* last

des of the, from the; contraction of **de** + **les**; some

dimanche *n.m.* Sunday

dire *v.* to say, to tell; **vouloir dire** to mean

donc *conj.* therefore, consequently

donner *v.* to give

dont *pron.* of which, whose

dormir *v.* to sleep
douche *n.f.* shower (bath)
douter *v.* to doubt
drôle *adj.* funny, droll
du of the, from the; contraction of **de** + **le**; some
dû *past participle of* **devoir**; ought to, must

eau *n.f.* water
école *n.f.* school; **à l'école** in (at, to) school; **une école de danse**
   dance school
écouter *v.* to listen (to)
écrire *v.* to write
écrivons *v. form of* **écrire**
égal, égaux, égale, égales *adj.* equal
église *n.f.* church
en *pron.* of it, of them, some of it, some of them; *prep.* in
encore *adv.* still, yet, again
encre *n.f.* ink
enregistrer *v.* to record (on a tape, record)
enseigner *v.* to teach
entendre *v.* to hear, to understand
enthousiasme *n.m.* enthusiasm
entre *prep.* between; *also a v. form of* **entrer (dans)** to enter (into)
envers *prep.* toward
environ *adv.* nearly, about
envoyer *v.* to send; **envoyer chercher** to send for
Espagne *n.f.* Spain
espagnol *n.m.* Spanish (language); **Espagnol, Espagnole** *n.* Spanish
   (person)
est *present Indicative of* **être**
Etats-Unis *n.m.pl.* United States
été *n.m.* summer; also *past participle of* **être**
être *v.* to be
étudiant, étudiante *n.m.* student
étudier *v.* to study
eu *past participle of* **avoir**

faim *n.f.* hunger; **avoir faim** to be hungry
faire *v.* to do, to make; **faire un voyage** to take a trip
falloir *v.* to be necessary; **il faut** it is necessary
faux, fausse *adj.* false

favori, favorite *adj.* favorite
femme *n.f.* woman; when possessive, wife; **ma femme** my wife
fête *n.f.* feast, holiday, party
feu *n.m.* fire; **le feu rouge** red light (traffic)
février *n.m.* February
fille *n.f.* daughter; **la jeune fille** girl
fils *n.m.* son
finir *v.* to finish, to end
forêt *n.f.* forest
fourchette *n.f.* fork
français *n.m.* French (language); **Français, Française** *n.* French (person)
franchement *adv.* frankly
frère *n.m.* brother
fromage *n.m.* cheese
fuir *v.* to flee, to run away; *past participle* **fui**

garçon *n.m.* boy
gâteau *n.m.* cake
gentil, gentille *adj.* nice, pleasant
gentiment *adv.* gently
gomme *n.f.* eraser (rubber)
grand, grande *adj.* great, big, large; **un grand magasin** department store
Grande Bretagne *n.f.* Great Britain
gris, grise *adj.* gray
gros, grosse *adj.* big, fat, large

heureusement *adv.* fortunately, happily
heureux, heureuse *adj.* happy
homme *n.m.* man
honneur *n.m.* honor
huître *n.f.* oyster

ici *adv.* here
île *n.f.* isle, island
immeuble *n.m.* (apartment) building
interrompre *v.* to interrupt
italien *n.m.* Italian (language); **Italien, Italienne** *n.* Italian (person)

janvier *n.m.* January
jeune *adj.* young
jeune fille *n.f.* girl

joli, jolie *adj.* pretty
jouer *v.* to play
jouet *n.m.* toy
jour *n.m.* day
journal *n.m.* newspaper
journée *n.f.* (all) day (long)

la *definite article, f.* the; *also direct object pronoun, f. sing.* it, her
laid, laide *adj.* ugly
laideur *n.f.* ugliness
laver *v.* to wash (something or someone); **se laver** *reflex. verb* to wash oneself
le *definite article, m.* the; *also direct object pronoun, m. sing.* it, him
lent, lente *adj.* slow
lentement *adv.* slowly
les *definite article, m. and f.* the; *also direct object pronoun, m. and f., pl.* them (people or things)
leur *possessive adj.* their; *also indirect object pron.* to them
lire *v.* to read; *past participle* **lu**
lit *n.m.* bed; *also present indicative, 3rd person sing. of* **lire**
livre *n.m.* book; **la livre** pound
Londres *n.m.* London
long, longue *adj.* long
longtemps *adv.* long time; **depuis longtemps** since a long time, for a long time
lorsque *adv.* when; *synonym of* **quand**
lui *indirect object pron., 3rd person sing.* to him, to her
lundi *n.m.* Monday

ma *possessive adj., f. sing.* my; **ma maison** my house
magasin *n.m.* store; **un grand magasin** department store
magazine *n.m.* magazine
maintenant *adv.* now
mais *conj.* but
maison *n.f.* house
malheur *n.m.* unhappiness
malheureusement *n.f.* unfortunately
manger *v.* to eat
marcher *v.* to walk, to march, to run (a machine)
mardi *n.m.* Tuesday
mars *n.m.* March
matin *n.m.* morning; **le matin** in the morning

médecin *n.m.* doctor
médecine *n.f.* medicine (profession)
médicament *n.m.* medicine (that you take)
meilleur, meilleure *adj.* better
mer *n.f.* sea
mère *n.f.* mother
mettre *v.* to put, to place; to put on (clothing)
mieux *adv.* better
monnaie *n.f.* change (money); coins
monsieur *n.m.* gentleman, sir, Mr.
mourir *v.* to die

naître *v.* to be born; *past participle* **né**
natation *n.f.* swimming
noir, noire *adj.* black
nom *n.m.* name
nouveau, nouvel, nouvelle *adj.* new

œil *n.m.* eye; **les yeux** eyes
œuf *n.m.* egg
oiseau *n.m.* bird
on *personal pron., 3rd person sing.* one (they)
oser *v.* to dare
ou *conj.* or; **où** *adv.* where
ouvrir *v.* to open; *past participle* **ouvert**

pain *n.m.* bread
papier *n.m.* paper
par *prep.* by; **par terre** on the floor, on the ground
parapluie *n.m.* umbrella
parc *n.m.* park
paresse *n.f.* laziness
paresseux, paresseuse *adj.* lazy
parler *v.* to talk, to speak
partir *v.* to leave; *past participle* **parti**
passer *v.* to spend (time); to go by, to pass by, to pass
pendant *prep.* during; **pendant que** *conj.* while
perdre *v.* to lose; *past participle* **perdu(e)(s)**
père *n.m.* father
perspicacité *n.f.* perspicacity, insight
peu (de) *adv.* little (of)

peur *n.f.* fear; **avoir peur** to be afraid, to feel afraid
peut *present indicative of* **pouvoir**
pied *n.m.* foot; **aller à pied** to walk
plage *n.f.* beach, seashore
pleuvoir *v.* to rain; *past participle* **plu**
plus *adv.* more; **plus de, plus que** more than
plusieurs *adv.* several
poule *n.f.* hen
poupée *n.f.* doll
pousser *v.* to push, to bud (flowers)
pouvoir *v.* to be able, can
précise *adj.* precise, precisely
prendre *v.* to take
presse *n.f.* press (printing)
public, publique *adj.* public
puis *adv.* then

quand *adv.* when; *synonym of* **lorsque**
quel, quelle, quels, quelles *adj.* which, what
quelque(s) *adj.* some; **quelque chose** something
quelquefois *adv.* sometimes
qui *pron.* who, whom
qui est-ce qui *pron.* who
quitter *v.* to leave (a person or place)
quoi *pron.* what (as obj. of a prep.); **avec quoi** with what

rang *n.m.* rank, row
restaurant *n.m.* restaurant
rire *v.* to laugh; *n.m.* laughter
robe *n.f.* dress
rose *n.f.* rose; *adj.* pink
rue *n.f.* street

samedi *n.m.* Saturday
sans *prep.* without
se *reflexive pron.* himself, herself, oneself
sec, sèche *adj.* dry
seize sixteen
semaine *n.f.* week
si *conj.* if
sœur *n.f.* sister

soir *n.m.* evening; **le soir** in the evening
son *n.m.* sound; *possessive adj.* his, her, its
sont *v. form of* **être**
sous *prep.* under
souvent *adv.* often
stylo *n.m.* pen
sucette *n.f.* lollipop; **sucer** *v.* to suck
sur *prep.* on

tenir *v.* to hold
thé *n.m.* tea
très *adv.* very
trop (de) *adv.* too much (of), too many (of)
trouver *v.* to find; **se trouver** *reflexive v.* to be located
tuer *v.* to kill

un *indefinite article, m. sing.* a, an (one); *fem.,* **une**

vacances *n.f.pl.* vacation; **les grandes vacances** summer vacation
vache *n.f.* cow
vais *present indicative of* **aller**
vendre *v.* to sell
venir *v.* to come
vent *n.m.* wind; **il fait du vent** it's windy
viande *n.f.* meat
vient *present indicative of* **venir**
vieux, vieil, vieille *adj.* old
vin *n.m.* wine
vingt twenty
voir *v.* to see; *past participle* **vu**
voyage *n.m.* trip; **faire un voyage** to take a trip, go on a trip; **Bon voyage!** Have a good trip!

y *adverbial pron.* there, in it, on it
yeux *n.m.* eyes; **l'œil** the eye

zèbre *n.m.* zebra

Index

Numbers refer to sections designated by the symbol § in this book.

à + **les** changes to **aux** §3.1
à, au, aux in idioms §12.2
about which §6.1–10
acheter §1.; §7.17
active voice §22.
adjectives §5.; §22; in an adverbial sense §5.4–7; with parts of the body & clothing §5.4–4
adverbs §8.; §22; of quantity §8.3–2
affirmative statement §22.
ago (**il y a** + length of time) §12.1
agreement of adjectives §5.2, §22.
agreement of subject and verb §7.1
agreement of verbs §7.1
aller fully conjugated in all the tenses §7.19; in idioms §12.2
all's well that ends well §6.1–9
amounts §16.
antecedent §6.1–13; §22; indefinite antecedent and subjunctive §7.15
antonyms (opposite meanings) §18.
any, some §3.3
anyone, anything §6.1–9
appeler (s') §7.17
apprendre §7.17
approximate amounts §16.
arithmetical expressions §16.
articles §3.
as . . . as §5.4–5
au from **à** + **le** §3.1
au, aux In idioms §12.2
auquel, auxquels, à laquelle, auxquelles §6.1–10
aussi . . . que §5.4–5
aux from **à** + **les** §3.1
auxiliary verbs **avoir, être** §7.3–1, §22.
avoir conjugated in all the tenses §7.19; in idioms §12.2
avoir, être as auxiliary verbs §7.1; §7.3–1
avoir verb (**parler**) conjugated in all the tenses in French and English §7.6

bas in idioms §12.2
beau, bel, belle, beaux §5.1
beaucoup (de) §8.3–2
bien in idioms §12.2
boire §7.17
bon, bonne §5.1; **bon** in idioms §12.2

ça §6.1–8; in idioms §12.2
capitalization §2.1
cardinal numbers §16, §22.
causative (causal) **faire** §7.14, §22.
ce (c'), ceci, cela, ça §6.1–8
ce, c'est in idioms §12.2
ce, cet, cette, ces §5.4–2
ce dont §6.1–13
ce que, ce qu' §6.1–13
ce qui §6.1–13
ceci, cela §6.1–8
cela in idioms §12.2
celui, celle, ceux, celles §6.1–8
cent §3.2, §16.
c'est + adjective + **à** + infinitive §6.1–14; in idioms §12.2
chez moi, chez toi, *etc.* §6.1–7
-ci (as in **celui-ci**) §6.1–8
clause §22.
cognates §19.
combien (de) §8.3–2
command (imperative) §7.8–15
commencer §7.17
common irregular past participles §7.2
common irregular present participles §7.4
comparative and superlative adjectives §5.4–5, §22.
comparative and superlative adverbs §8.3–3, §22.
complex sentence §22.
compound past tense (**passé composé**) §7.8–8
compound sentence §22.
comprendre, entendre §7.11, §7.17
conditional perfect §7.8–12

233

conditional present §7.8–5
conduire §7.17
conjugation §22.
conjunctions §10.; with subjunctive §7.15, §22.
connaître, savoir §7.11, §7.17
contrary to fact (if clause) §7.10

dans and **en** + length of time §9.1
dates §13.1
days of the week §13.2
de + le changes to **du** §3.1
de + les changes to **des** §3.1
de, du, d' in idioms §12.2
de la, du, de l', des §3.1, §3.3
declarative sentence §22.
definite articles §3.1, §22.
demonstrative adjectives §5.4–2, §22.
demonstrative pronouns §6.1–8, §22.
dependent clause §22.
depuis, depuis combien de temps, depuis quand §12.1
des from **de + les** §3.1
descriptive adjectives §5.4–1, §22.
desquels, desquelles §6.1–10
devoir §7.11, §7.17
direct object noun §22.
direct object pronouns §6.1–2, §22.
disjunctive pronouns §6.1–7, §22.
division of words §2.3
dont §6.1–13
double object pronouns §6.1–4
du from **de + le** §3.1
duquel, desquels, de laquelle, desquelles §6.1–10

écrire §7.17
en §6.1–5
en + present participle §7.4
en and **dans** + length of time §9.1
en in idioms §12.2
ending of a verb §22.
entendre, comprendre §7.11, §7.17
envers and **vers** §9.2
est-ce in idioms §12.2
est-ce que §21.
être as auxiliary verb §7.1, §7.3–1

être fully conjugated in all the tenses §7.19
être in idioms §12.2
être verb **(venir)** conjugated in all the tenses in French and English §7.7
eux §6.1–7

faire causative (causal) §7.14
faire fully conjugated in all the tenses §7.19
faire in idioms §12.2
faut (falloir) §7.11, §7.17
feminine §22.
fol, fou §5.1
fractions §16.
future perfect tense §7.8–11
future tense §7.8–4

gender of nouns §4.1, §22.
gerund §22.

hour of the day §14.
how to ask a question §21.
how to form the plural of nouns §4.2
how to make a verb negative §7.18

idioms and idiomatic expressions §12.
if (si) clause §7.10
il est + adjective + **de** + infinitive §6.1–15
il y a + length of time + **que** §12.1
imperative (command) §7.8–15, §22.
imperfect indicative tense §7.8–2
imperfect subjunctive tense §7.8–7
in the morning, in the afternoon, in the evening §3.1
indefinite articles §3.2, §22.
indefinite pronouns §6.1–9, §22.
independent clause §22.
indicative mood §22.
indirect object noun §22.
indirect object pronouns §6.1–3, §22.
infinitives §7.13, §22.
interjection §22.
interrogative adjectives §5.4–3, §22.
interrogative adverbs §8.3–1, §22.
interrogative pronouns §6.1–10, §22.

interrogative statements §21.
intransitive verbs §7.3–3, §22.
inverted form of question §21.
irregular comparative and
  superlative adjectives §5.4–5
irregular comparative and
  superlative adverbs §8.3–3
irregular past participles §7.2
irregular present participles §7.4
irregular verb §22.

jouer à, jouer de §7.5

-là (as in **celui-là**) §6.1–8
la leur, les leurs §6.1–11
la mienne, la tienne, la sienne
  §6.1–11
la nôtre, la vôtre §6.1–11
laisser §7.11
**laquelle, lequel, lesquelles,
  lesquels** §6.1–10, §6.1–13
le, la, l', les §3.1
le (la) nôtre, le (la) vôtre §6.1–11
le leur, les leurs §6.1–11
le mien, le tien, le sien §6.1–11
le neuter pronoun §6.1–16
**lequel, lesquels, laquelle,
  lesquelles** §6.1–10, §6.1–13
les leurs, la leur §6.1–11
**les miennes, les tiennes, les
  siennes** §6.1–11
les miens, les tiens, les siens
  §6.1–11
les nôtres, les vôtres §6.1–11
less . . . than §5.4–5
leur (le), leurs (les) §6.1–11
leur, leurs §5.4–4
limiting adjective §22.
lui, leur §6.1–3

main clause §22.
masculine §22.
me, te, se §6.1–12
meilleur, mieux §5.4–6
mien (le), tien (le), sien (le)
  §6.1–11
mienne (la), tienne (la), sienne (la)
  §6.1–11

**miennes (les), tiennes (les),
  siennes (les)** §6.1–11
miens (les), tiens (les), siens (les)
  §6.1–11
mieux §5.4–6; in idioms §12.2
mine, yours, ours, theirs, *etc.* §6.1–11
moi, toi, soi §6.1–7
moins . . . que §5.4–5
mon, ma, mes §5.4–4
months of the year §13.3
mood of verbs §22.
more . . . than §5.4–5
most §5.4–5
my, your, his, her, *etc.* §5.4–4
myself, yourself, herself, himself,
  ourselves, *etc.* §6.1–11

negations of verbs §7.18
negative constructions §11.1, §22.
neither . . . nor §3.1
neuter §22.
neuter pronoun **le** §6.1–16
nobody, no one §6.1–9
non in idioms §12.2
not as . . . as §5.4–5
not one, not any, none §6.1–9
nôtre (la), vôtre (la) §6.1–11
notre, nos §5.4–4
nôtres (les), vôtres (les) §6.1–11
nouns §4, §22.
numbers §16, §22.

of whom, of which §6.1–13
on §6.1–1, §6.1–9
on Saturdays . . . §3.1
on the telephone §6.1–10
only §3.3
order of words in French sentences
  §11.
ordinal numbers §16, §22.
orthographical (spelling) changes in
  verb forms §7.17, §22.
où §6.1–13
oui and **si** §8.4

par in idioms §12.2
parler conjugated in all the tenses in
  French and English §7.6
participles §7.1, §7.2, §7.4

partir, sortir §7.11, §7.17
partitive §3.3, §22.
parts of body and articles of
  clothing with definite article §3.1,
  §5.4–4
parts of speech §3.
passé composé §7.8–8, §22.
passé simple §7.8–3
passive voice §7.9, §22.
past anterior tense §7.8–10
past indefinite tense §7.8–8, §22.
past infinitive §7.13
past participle of an **avoir** verb
  with a preceding direct object §7.1
past participles §7.1, §7.2, §22.
past subjunctive §7.8–13
pendant §9.3
penser à §7.5
person (1st, 2nd, 3rd) §22.
personal pronoun §22.
pluperfect indicative §7.8–9
pluperfect subjunctive §7.8–14
plural of nouns §4.2, §22.
plus in idioms §12.2; **plus . . . que**
  §5.4–5
position of adjectives §5.3
position of double object pronouns
  §6.1–4
position of words in French
  sentences §11.
possessive adjectives §5.4–4, §22.
possessive pronouns §6.1–11
pouvoir §7.11, §7.17
predicate §22.
prepositions §9, §22; with verbs
  §7.5
present indicative tense §7.8–1, §22.
present participles §7.4, §22.
present subjunctive §7.8–6
pronouns §6, §22.
pronunciation of French sounds
  §1, §2.
punctuation marks §2.2

qu'est-ce que §6.1–10
qu'est-ce que c'est que cela?
  §6.1–8

qu'est-ce qui §6.1–10
que, qu' §6.1–10, §6.1–13
quel, quelle, quels, quelles §5.4–3;
  quel, quelle in idioms §12.2
quelque chose in idioms §12.2
questions, how to ask §21.
qui §6.1–10, §6.1–13
qui est-ce que, qui est-ce qui
  §6.1–10
quitter §7.11
quoi §6.1–10; **quoi** in idioms §12.2

reflexive pronouns and reflexive
  verbs §6.1–12, §7.1, §7.3–1, §22.
regular verb §22.
relative pronouns §6.1–13, §22.
rien in idioms §12.2

sa, son, ses §5.4–4
savoir, connaître §7.11, §7.17
se §6.1–12
seasons of the year §13.4
sentence §22.
si and **oui** §8.4
si (if) clause §7.10
simple past tense §7.8–3
simple sentence §22.
some, a few 6.1–9
some, any §3.3
something, someone, somebody
  §6.1–9
son, sa, ses §5.4–4
sortir, partir §7.11, §7.17
spelling irregularities of some
  common verb forms §7.17
stem of verb §22.
subject §22.
subject pronouns §6.1–1
subjunctive §7.15, §22.
subordinate clause §22.
suffixes §19.
summary of verb tenses and moods
  §7.16
superlative of adjectives §5.4–5,
  §22.
superlative of adverbs §8.3–3, §22.
syllables §2.3
synonyms (similar meanings) §17.

tant in idioms §12.2
te §6.1–12
telling time §14.
tenses and moods §7.8, §7.16, §22.
that, those §5.4–2
the one, the ones §6.1–8
there is, there are **(il y a)** §12.1; **y** in
    idiomatic expressions §12.2
this, these §5.4–2
time expressions §14.2
to Canada, to France, to the airport,
    to the United States §3.1
to which one, to which ones §6.1–10
ton, ta, tes §5.4–4
tous, tout, toute in idioms §12.2
transitive verbs §7.3–2, §22.
tricky words ("false friends") §20.

un, une, des §3.2

venir conjugated in all the tenses in
    French and English §7.7
verb negations §7.18
verb tenses and moods §7.8, §7.16
verb tenses and moods in French
    with English equivalents §7.19
verbs §7, §22; stem §22.
verbs and prepositions §7.5
verbs conjugated with **avoir** §7.3–1;
    §7.6

verbs conjugated with **être** §7.3–1;
    §7.7
verbs with special meanings §7.11,
    §7.12
vers and **envers** §9.2
vocabularies §17, §18, §20.
voici, voilà + length of time + **que**
    §12.1
vôtre (la, le), nôtre (la, le)
    §6.1–11
votre, vos §5.4–4
vôtres (les), nôtres (les)
    §6.1–11
vouloir §7.11, §7.17
voyager §7.17

weather expressions §15.
what, which §5.4–3
what a . . . ! §3.2; §5.4–3
what happened? §6.1–10
which, what §5.4–3
which one, which ones §6.1–10
whoever §6.1–9
word division §2.3
word order of elements in French
    sentences §11.

y §6.1–6; position of **y** §11.2–§11.5;
    il y a §12.1; in idioms §12.2